Teaching Human Beings

Teaching Human Beings

101 Subversive Activities
for the Classroom

By Jeffrey Schrank

Beacon Press   Boston

Copyright © 1972 by Jeffrey Schrank
Library of Congress catalog card number: 73-179154
International Standard Book Number: 0-8070-3176-3 (hardcover)
0-8070-3177-1 (paperback)
Beacon Press books are published under the auspices
of the Unitarian Universalist Association
Published simultaneously in Canada by Saunders of Toronto, Ltd.
All rights reserved
Printed in the United States of America

To Louise

CONTENTS

Here is Edward Bear, coming downstairs now, bump, bump, bump, on the back of his head, behind Christopher Robin. It is, as far as he knows, the only way of coming downstairs, but sometimes he feels that there really is another way, if only he could stop bumping for a moment and think of it.

A. A. Milne, *Winnie-the-Pooh*

Our capacity to think, except in the service of what we are dangerously deluded in supposing is our self-interest and in conformity with common sense, is pitifully limited: our capacity even to see, hear, touch, taste and smell is so shrouded in veils of mystification that an intensive discipline of unlearning is necessary for anyone before one can begin to experience the world afresh with innocence, truth and love.

R. D. Laing, *The Politics of Experience*

NTRODUCTION

I'm not sure if society should be deschooled or if society's values should be taken out of schools. I'm not sure if compulsory education is a pillar of our country's virtue or a contributing factor in the nation's eventual downfall. I'm not sure if schools can become a center of change for society or if society must change before schools.

There are many other controversial questions surrounding schools about which I'm not yet sure. So I decided to write a book about things of which I am sure. I'm sure there are thousands of human beings with the label *teacher* who earn a living in schools at least nine months of the year. I'm also sure they need ideas to help prevent school from handicapping kids. So here is a collection (101 is a conservative guess) of ideas that have worked for me during the past four years. With a little creativity and adaptation, they can work with grade-school classes, as well as adults, although they were dreamed up with a high school audience in mind.

Teaching Human Beings is not another book demonstrating how harmful the schools are; this has already been well documented. It is rather a book which explores what possible good can come from throwing from fifteen to forty teen-agers and one adult together for about 175 hours a year. What good does happen is likely to be subversive (thanks to Postman and Weingartner) to the traditional goals of schooling. But this isn't a book about schooling; it's about educating.

There is no question that a revolution in education is needed and is on its way. This book is what-to-do-until-the-revolution-comes.

The "subversive activities" outlined in the following pages are the sort of small changes that might lead to more significant reforms. They can be done without firing the principal, burning down the athletic office, or spilling eight thousand marbles in the hallway one minute before the bell rings. They open up lines of communication, enable students and teachers to see each other as human beings, and demand that adults in schools stop teaching-to and start learning-with.

Behind many of the activities described in this book is another idea which requires a basic attitudinal change. A premise upon which schools are built is that kids must be taught what they don't know; schools are based on the assumption that ignorance is bad. Fair enough. But the acceptance of this neglects another problem. What kids do "know" is just as, if not more, dangerous than what they don't know. This is especially true if they have already been subjected to six or more years of compulsory schooling. So running through this cookbook of ideas is the theme of "unlearning." Starvation is a cause of death to be pitied and fought but far more people die because of what they do eat than die of what they lack. The same is true of education. Ignorance may be more dramatic, but knowledge is just as dangerous.

By the time a child becomes a teen-ager and enters high school he is filled with myths, misconceptions, fears, and doubts which schooling and parents have forced upon him. One role of the activities in this book is to help the student see the possible dangers in what he already has learned and now takes for granted. Some knowledge which a vast number of teens have learned and which desperately needs to be unlearned is: I am not important; my feelings cannot be trusted and should be controlled; I need permission to do things; adults usually know better; I am controlled by outside forces; I must hide my real self; learning is something others give to me; I must become what others want me to.

It is impossible to separate change in the schools from change in society. Educational critics and radical reformers are asking schools to become agents of change instead of preservers of the status quo. They are asking schools to change the culture; they are not asking schools to do a better job within the existing culture. If that can be done, I don't know. What I do know is that there are teachers and group leaders out there fully capable of enabling people, sometimes called students, to help themselves grow and learn. They have learned that the river can't be pushed, that love and caring are more important than any grade or degree, and that even schools can be places of growth. This book is for them and others who wish to move in the same direction.

Teaching Human Beings

SENSE EDUCATION

Learn to apprehend the world with unobstructed senses. . . . If the doors of perception were cleansed, everything would appear to man as it is—infinite.

William Blake

Schools teach non-sense. They claim to train and instruct, perhaps even educate, the mind but make no effort to educate the senses. They do not teach how to observe, listen, touch, taste, or smell, in spite of the considerable evidence which indicates that the senses can indeed be educated. Such neglect is not the fault of "mindless" men who run school systems but merely an accurate reflection of the fact that our culture does not place a high value on sensuality and sensory awareness.

Developing the potential present in the senses would appear to be a natural function of education in most any culture. In many primitive cultures it is, but in the civilized and developed countries the senses are most often neglected. In these same "developed" cultures there are pressures which tend to encourage stunting the growth of sensory awareness—pollution, increasing noise levels, artificial environments, standardization, a rapid pace of living, repetition, and standardized and chemical pseudo foods. All these forces tend to lessen the joy of sensation.

We are reasonably certain that the senses can be educated but are not sure how this can be done, or even if it can be done in the context

1

of institutional schooling. The exercises which follow are aimed at an adolescent or adult audience and help teach that the senses are sources of as yet undiscovered enjoyment. To be truly effective, sense education would have to start at the preschool level and be a consistent part of education through life.

If schools were ever to succeed in developing the sense potential of students the culture would be changed. As Charles Reich points out in *The Greening of America*

> No person with a strongly developed aesthetic sense, a love of nature, a passion for music, a desire for reflection, or a strong marked independence, could possibly be happy or contented in a factory or white-collar job. Hence these characteristics must be snuffed out in school.

A change in the sense awareness of a society is one of the most profound changes a culture could possibly undergo. If we had more sensitive ears and noses, our environment would not only seem different; it would actually be different, despite the fact that the things in it do not change physically. If sensuality were valued in the culture and successfully taught in the schools for ten years, there could possibly be social changes that would make the American Revolution seem like a series of minor political reforms.

HEARING

There's an old expression about "hearing what you want to hear" that demonstrates a true psychological insight. Hearing is a biological process that needs no training; listening is a psychological process that is learned. There are many sounds we hear but do not listen to simply because we have been taught to disregard them.

In François Truffaut's film *Wild Child*, a boy, abandoned and left in the woods as dead as a child, is found leading the life of an animal. The boy had raised himself without human contact for twelve years. After his accidental discovery and capture he was sent to a home for deaf mutes, since it was believed he could neither hear nor talk. One of the captors related to the doctor that he had noticed the boy react to the sound of a nut cracking behind him and so couldn't be deaf. To test the boy's hearing the doctor slammed a door behind the boy— there was no reaction.

The "wild child" did indeed have a sense of hearing, but his sense education had been provided by the sounds of the woods. He did not react to the noise of the door because it was a sound he was not educated to listen for. Years later, after much formal training, his sense of hearing became normal, meaning that he reacted to those same stimuli that other eighteenth-century Frenchmen considered worth recognizing. His training also made him unable to detect the muted sounds of nature to which he was once attuned. His "education" consisted largely in retraining the senses rather than in freeing them to develop their full potential.

The kind of selective hearing developed by the wild child is different only in choice of sounds from that of technological man. Technological man has developed an almost remarkable ability to disregard many sounds—a psychological "earlid." Sound plays a minor role in the sense lives of Americans, compared to primitive people. As J. C. Carothers reports in the November 1959 issue of *Psychiatry* magazine, ". . . for Europeans, in general, 'seeing is believing,' for rural Africans reality seems to reside far more in what is heard and what is said."

It is likely that our visual bias is responsible for the lack of education for listening. The school curriculum reflects the visual bias (notice that the word "reflects" seems more natural than the word "echoes") of the culture. It is not surprising that teachers complain of student inability to listen or follow directions or to conduct group discussions. Schools teach nonlistening. Not to teach listening is to teach that it is not important.

The exercises which follow are not the answer to a visual bias or a total school neglect of listening. They do serve to provide insights into the listening process and have been used to make students aware of their tendency to hear but not listen.

Listening Exercises
Have everyone be absolutely quiet, and allow one or two minutes for listening to sounds not usually heard in the room. Be aware of the "layers" of sound in the room. Discuss the experience. Talk about what would happen if there were a machine which could turn off each layer of sound as it was noticed until there was absolute silence.

Have a discussion about how you deal with noise and silence in your own life.

Find a stereo test record that has various tones ranging from a low of around 20 c.p.s. to a high of 20,000 c.p.s. A man announces each tone. Play the record on a school phonograph; how many tones do you hear?

Have a tape or record and a series of recorders or phonographs of increasingly higher quality. Start with the worst machine and work to the best, playing the same record or tape on each. Notice with each playing the sounds that are heard for the first time.

Try "Did You Hear What I Hear?" on page 145.

Do a hearing identification test using taped or live sounds which students have to identify without seeing the source. Discuss how sound and sight work together.

Using as high a quality tape recorder as possible, tape each student's speaking for about one minute. Play the tape back, and have students react to the sound of their own voice. Discuss the voice sounds in relation to self-image. The most common reaction to this experience is for students to feel that their voice "doesn't sound like that" but to realize that everyone else's voice is accurately reproduced.

Tendencies in ourselves are often more noticeable when carried to their extreme. This exercise is designed to promote the utmost frustration and to discourage listening. Have the group break into trios, and assign roles for each to play and a problem to solve (e.g., parent-child-teacher roles with the problem being low grades in math). Instruct each person to make it a point not to listen to each other but to discuss the problem at hand. Go around to the trios during the "discussion" to make sure there is no listening. This exercise ends when the noise level becomes too high. Discuss the feelings and dynamics involved and compare them to real situations.

Try the tape series *Effective Communication: A Tape Guide to Improved Awareness and Self-Expression* (Argus Communications, 3505 N. Ashland Ave., Chicago, Ill. 60657). This four-tape series includes activities (it is not a lecture series) in which the teacher participates as a group member while the tape gives the instructions. Tape titles are:

"The Art of Listening," "Feelings," "Mannerisms and Body Talk," and "Attacking and Defending." The series presents games and discussions designed to improve and create greater awareness of the art of listening. The four tapes (cassette or open reel) and study guide and other needed materials sell in kit form for $27.50. A sample recording and brochure are available free upon request.

Have students form groups of two. The two should select one as the speaker and one as an echo. The speaker simply talks for one minute while the echo attempts to repeat his words. Ideally, a perfect pair would sound like one person speaking in two voices. More practically, a gap of less than a second can be maintained with a little practice. Have students speak slowly for a start, and distinctly. Switch positions. Combine two pairs, and try the echoing with a group of four. If possible, try to build into one large circle with one person speaking and the others acting as his verbal mirrors. The exercise provides an experience in total concentration on what others are saying.

An old standby which often demonstrates the lack of listening which passes for normal is the rumor game. Divide the group into teams of about six to ten persons each. Have each team line up, and give the first person in each team a piece of paper with a very short story to read (the story could be a newspaper clipping or a made-up story of an accident, crime, etc.) no longer than 200 words. The first person in each team should read the paper and give it back to the group leader. He then tells the story as well as he can remember it to the second person in the group, who in turn tells it to the third. Each team does this by whispering. The last person in each team then writes down his version of the story, and each final version is compared to the original story. Discuss where changes in the story took place and why.

SIGHT

Just as there is a difference between hearing and listening, there is also a distinction between sight and observation. Hearing can be improved by a mechanical hearing aid, but listening remains unchanged. Sight can be improved by glasses or contact lenses, but observation resists mechanical aids. Observation is to sight what listening is to hearing.

Observation, like listening, is a learned process. As I sit here now typing three days before spring officially begins, I look outside and observe that it's snowing. To me snow is snow. Any white stuff that falls from the sky during winter I label snow. To an Eskimo, for whom snow is a far more vital part of the environment than it is for me, snow is any one of forty-eight entirely different things. Eskimos have learned to see that white stuff that falls from the sky as forty-eight different things. To them snow on one day is not the same as snow the next day. When I stop to think about it, I realize that there are huge fluffy flakes and tiny wind-driven pellets of snow, there are heavy snow and light snow and probably hundreds of varieties of snow. Since snow is not too important to me I lump them all together in one word—*snow*. Therefore, I never learn to appreciate fully the varieties of snow as does the Eskimo. An Eskimo sitting next to me now would actually see something different if he looked out the window. Observation is a learned process.

If we were to become Eskimos we would have to reeducate our powers of observation. The first settlers in the New World had to retrain their sense of sight in order to survive. Now we are asking if sight can be educated for greater awareness and enjoyment rather than for survival. We tend to be sensual clods when it comes to vision, seeing much but observing little.

A deck of cards is symbolic of our approach to observation. Right now, without looking at any cards, tell which king has only one eye showing. Don't know? Get out a deck of cards and spread out the kings. The king of diamonds is shown in profile and only one eye is visible. Look at the four kings and find their differences. The king of diamonds has the distinction of being the only king with an ax—the others have swords. Look at the other picture cards. All the Queens are holding flowers, and the costume of each carries the motif of her suit. The Jack of Hearts holds a leaf while the Jack of Diamonds is the only one with a weapon and only the Spade holds a strange-looking knot.

In spite of the fact that these cards have been seen probably hundreds, if not thousands of times, their differences were never noticed. What is symbolic about this lack of observation is that the reason the details have escaped notice is that card players look at the cards only to determine their values, to label and classify them. In seeking their label the card player misses their differences, their individuality.

Such is our behavior in regard to many aspects of the world of vision.

Even in "art education" classes teachers seem more interested in labeling pictures and schools of art than in simply enjoying beauty. Newspapers further the labelphobia by giving art attention mainly when a painting is sold for some huge sum of money.

The exercises which follow will not bring eyesight closer to the 20/20 level, but they might help create an awareness of the enjoyment that is normally missing from our world of observation.

Observation Exercises
Try the "Non-Sense Walk" on page 156.

Try "Personality Mirror" on page 147.

Try "Eyes" on page 144.

Look around the room for one minute and find some things you have never "observed" before. If the room has windows try the same, looking outside. Share the "finds" and talk about the experience.

Meet outside, if possible, and look at the clouds, trees, grass, or buildings. Have some time for silent observation and sharing of insights.

Have a group arrange to watch the sun rise or set or watch the stars.

Have everyone mill around the room, walking aimlessly. Call a freeze after a minute or less, and have each person choose the person closest as partner. Partners should face and look each other over front to back and top to bottom. If the group contains both sexes a cultural bias immediately manifests itself—any intensive look is considered sexual in nature. This might cause nervous giggling; if so it would be a clue for later discussion.

After the two have looked each other over, have them face away from each other and change three things about themselves—jewelry, buttons, hair, clothing, etc. After this is done they should turn back and try to identify the three changes in the other person.

After this, mill around again, freeze with a new partner, and try changing six things. Discuss the experience if desirable.

Show a sense film such as any described in the filmography at the end of this chapter.

Stage a "surprise" event. Have some person not in the class enter the room to make an announcement, call someone out of the room, start an argument, or simply walk across the room and leave. After the outsider has left, ask the class for an accurate description of the person in writing. Ask specific questions, such as color of hair, eyes, height, clothing. Compare the descriptions with the correct answers, and discuss the experience.

Have everyone describe something they have seen hundreds of times but taken for granted. Choose something that affords immediate comparison such as the back wall, the corridor, the front of the building, the person in the corner.

Find and present several optical illusions. Discuss why they deceive.

Meditate on the speed of light. The sunlight which we see came from the sun eight minutes ago; stars in the night sky are seen as they existed thousands of years ago. The sun might have exploded six minutes ago, and we wouldn't know it; many stars in the night sky don't exist anymore.

Hold a class with everyone blindfolded.

Demonstrate the blind spot which exists in the normal field of vision by drawing this figure on a blackboard or bulletin board:

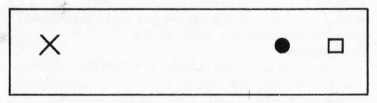

Close the left eye and look at the figure. Focus the right eye on the X and slowly move away from the figure (in a room with many desks have each person draw the figure on paper and move the paper away from the eye) until the circle disappears. Keep moving until the circle reappears and the square vanishes and comes back into view. Try to explain what happens, or allow someone to research the phenomenon.

Discuss how we are a visual culture where "seeing is believing," where wise men are "seers," where we say "I see what you mean." Discuss what happens when the sense of sight is cut off or overloaded—hypnotism, hallucinations, dreams, daydreams, illusions. Compare personal experiences.

TOUCH

DON'T TOUCH. Once a warning from parents to children eyeing expensive figurines perched on a fragile end table, the command "don't touch" has become a cultural mandate, a warning sign nailed over the whole country.

"Grown men shouldn't have to play in the mud" headlines an ad for International Nickel's new stadium domes. The two-page spread shows mud-soaked professional football players. Maybe they shouldn't have to play pro football in the mud, but hardly a burly lineman out there didn't at one time enjoy playing in the mud or even making mud pies; but no more. Most of the mud slingers have grown up and turned into spectators; a few still play the game but only for money and fame. Why have these men traded the cool oozing sensuality of mud for a one-year contract to perform on artificial grass in an air-conditioned and sealed stadium?

There is joy in the feel of mud, a sensual pleasure in being unprotected in a warm summer rain, in touching richly textured surfaces, in feeling the warmth and touch of other bodies, in the glow of real firelight, in the freedom of grass beneath the feet and between the toes, in the feel of food, and in the many sensations gained by reaching out to touch the world little by little. Ask any small kid.

That same little kid can also tell what happens when he innocently tries to enjoy this touching. He hears that he should not go out into the rain because he'll catch cold, should wear shoes because he might get cut feet, should not touch the other kids because it's "naughty" (it's OK, however, if he's a boy and the touching can be labeled fighting), should eat politely with utensils, and when in doubt should keep his hands to himself. He concludes there must be something wrong with the pleasures of touch or at least that it isn't worth the hassle. So he matures and loses touch.

He even learns, without a word being said, to build an invisible bubble around himself about eighteen inches from his skin. When another person enters this bubble, except in very carefully regulated circumstances, he considers it an attack and retreats or stages his own subtle counterattack. He learns that every-body has a bubble just like his and he survives nicely in his own personal space.

Freed from the pain and joys of touching he is able to cope with normal aloofness, little contact with other human beings, plastic-vinyl-veneer surfaces that are slick and cold, and even schoolroom desks and business suits and bras and girdles. As a teen-ager he would like to be cuddled (although he might not realize the real need) but has been taught that only by sexualizing this need can it be culturally acceptable to be physically handled. And his sexuality leads him into more problems.

He will grow old very likely never learning the full joys of the sense of touch. He will likely marry, produce children whom he will handle sparingly and in a scrupulously nonsexual manner, and raise them with strong defenses against a "don't touch" world.

Touch Exercises
Read the book *Sense Relaxation: Below Your Mind* by Bernard Gunther (New York: Collier Books, 1968) and try the program outlined. Adapt some of the ideas to classroom use.

Have everyone imagine himself dressed in his best clothes for a job interview. Have him imagine the pressure points in the clothing he's wearing. How do the clothes make him feel? Discuss what this says about our culture in terms of the expression "Clothes make the man." Discuss changes in fashion and why work and clothes which feel uncomfortable seem to go together.

Discuss going barefoot. Personal experiences, why or why not, parents' attitudes. Many public buildings put up signs outlawing bare feet. Discuss if there might be reasons beyond health laws for this practice.

Discuss how our culture deals with the problem of how and when people are allowed to touch each other. What would happen if at a school assembly the speaker asked everyone to hold the hand of the person sitting nearest him?

Pass objects around the group to be felt while blindfolded. If the group is too large divide into smaller groups of about eight. Pass objects such as a grape, apple, rock, cotton, rubber ball, golf ball. The object of the exercise is to experience how the objects feel—temperature, hardness, weight, texture, shape. The exercise could be made into an identification game if needed or desired.

Discuss how school furniture (desks) feels. Design furniture based primarily on its ability to make the user feel good.

Discuss the use of the word *touch* in expressions such as "out of touch," "touching experience," "he's touched."

Have everyone shake the hand of everyone else (or at least of some people). Discuss how people communicate through a handshake. Have people demonstrate the various messages which can be sent through a handshake such as "I'm the boss here," or "I'm scared."

Show and discuss the film *Invisible Walls* described on page 25.

Provide each person in the group with a potato. Make sure the potatoes are nearly uniform in size. Sit the group on the floor in a circle if possible; if the group is over twenty divide into two or more smaller groups. Give the group about three minutes to get to know their own potato visually—notice its shape, contours, imperfections, etc. After three minutes allow another two or three for learning how the potato feels without looking at it. Have the group split into pairs, and have each person introduce his potato to the other person, pointing out its uniqueness and allowing the other to feel and see the differences. Next combine two or four members to form a small circle, and have each member introduce his potato. Finally, gather the potatoes from the entire group, and mix them in the center of the circle. Redistribute the potatoes randomly, and have the group pass the potatoes around without looking at them. When a person has his own potato he places it in front of himself but continues to pass around other potatoes as they come to him. The exercise stops when each person has his own potato. Discuss the experience afterwards.

Have the group mill around with eyes closed or blindfolded. Without use of sight or sound each person should pick a partner. No one should know who his partner is. Have the two partners clasp and feel each other's hands. Tell them to express strength and tenderness using only the hand clasp. Tell the partners to feel each other's arms and shoulders and then gently explore the other's head and face. Encourage them to experience both what they are feeling and what is being felt. The exercise should be done in silence with the mood being one of reverence. Encourage relaxation and enjoyment of feelings. When finished have the two partners open eyes or remove each other's blindfolds and look at each other, still in silence, for a few seconds. Discuss feelings and reactions.

TASTE

Taste, like the other senses, has fallen victim to increasing standardization. In order to sell food to a large number of people, which a corporation must do to survive, the food must offend no one. The path the food industry has followed has been to sell to the lowest common denominator of taste by adding chemicals to cut costs and give artificial flavor and color.

After eating enough pseudo foods consumers begin to think that such tastelessness is the norm. They seldom, if ever, find a meal a rich sensual pleasure. They eat quickly, failing to savor each mouthful, since they assume there is little to taste. The old belief that produces a longing for food the way grandma used to make it may be more than mere nostalgia as taste is sacrificed to economics and convenience.

Preservatives are added to food often with more of an eye to money than taste. Two of the most common, BHA and BHT, find their way into everything from orange juice concentrate to doughnuts. Such preservatives add nothing to the taste of food, and some people claim they deaden the taste. The consumer can be sure that baked goods preserved with BHA and BHT can be eaten two days or two months after they leave the ovens and still taste like flavored paste.

Not only do chemicals in food affect flavor, but many are added without sufficient testing for their long-term effects. As Pulitzer Prize-winning journalist William Longgood states in *The Poisons in Your Food:*

> By means of propaganda, modern advertising techniques and a host of provocative names for toxic substances, people not only have accepted poisons in food but even consider them superior to natural products. They have accepted the false thesis that poisons cease to be harmful simply because they are taken in small quantities.

Those who eat only organic food (grown without chemicals) are considered health nuts or at least slightly weird. In reality, the average consumer who daily eats dozens of unknown and often untested chemicals could be considered a chemical freak. The average American consumes quantities of monosodium glutamate, calcium phosphate, sodium citrate, sodium silico-aluminate, dipotassium phosphate, butylated hydroxytoluene, propyl gallate, methyl polysilicone, and hundreds of other chemicals without any knowledge of their effects on taste or health.

Taste itself is a strange sense. There are those who practically dismiss taste as being secondary to smell. They even suggest that taste makes a relatively minor contribution to the joy of eating. "Taste is 90 percent smell," they conclude. "All you can taste of a steak is whether it's salty or not." Much of what they say is true, but taste nevertheless remains a crucial sense.

Exactly how crucial is suggested by the experience of a patient in a New York hospital whose case has become a classic in medical annals. The patient, Tom, drank some burning hot clam chowder that caused his esophagus to close. A tube was surgically implanted in his stomach through which he was to feed himself. But Tom remained poorly nourished, underweight and almost constantly hungry, no matter how good the food looked or smelled. Finally a system was devised that allowed him to taste the food, and from then on his appetite was healthy and his growth normal.

In another study, groups of servicemen were served pills at mealtime with all the nutritional value contained in the food eaten by the other servicemen on the normal diet. Drastic declines in morale were observed in the men deprived of the color, taste, and feel of a plate full of food three times a day.

There must be room somewhere in the curriculum for a unit on taste. Most schools state in their written objectives they are interested in the "whole person," "developing humane traits," "richness of life," etc., so certainly taste falls into the realm of the school.

Taste Exercises

Discuss why some people find a certain food enjoyable while others consider it almost unfit to eat. In the course of the discussion introduce the idea that many substances which Westerners reject as food are perfectly capable of providing nourishment—horses, dogs, cats, rats, snakes, caterpillars, and insects, as well as human flesh. As Ina Corinne Brown points out in her very readable introduction to anthropology *Understanding Other Cultures,* "To the orthodox Muslim our use of pork is revolting, and to the orthodox Hindu, the thought of eating beef is almost as horrifying as the thought of eating human flesh is to us. To many people a crisply roasted grasshopper is more palatable than a raw oyster. East Africans find eggs nauseating, and Chinese students have sometimes become ill at seeing people drink milk."

Have some food (a loaf of homemade bread would be excellent) which everyone could taste. Have them hold the food in the mouth until liquid before swallowing. Have a tasting party in which food is appreciated for its full taste. Try tasting and identifying various foods while blindfolded. Compare pseudo foods to real foods. Try organic food. Eat blindfolded. Try comparing homemade bread with store-bought bread.

Blindfold two volunteers, and give them a tasting test. Tell them they cannot touch the food but can smell and taste it. At one point in the test have the volunteers bite into an apple or potato slice while holding a cut onion near the nose. See if they believe they have eaten an onion. Most people hold their breath when eating food and have to be encouraged to smell the food first.

Bring some unusual food to try—octopus, crickets, seaweed cookies, hot peppers, soul food, etc. Have everyone try the foods and discuss his own likes and dislikes. Compare foods most commonly universally liked and disliked. Propose that food preferences are learned from childhood experiences and can be changed.

Have students read ingredients labels on frozen, canned, and packaged foods. Research the chemical ingredients.

SMELL

If you are troubled by a constant stream of elephants plodding through your classroom or home, a knowledge of osmics will help solve the problem. Osmics is the science of smell, and any study of osmics can tell you that the solution to the elephant problem is camels. It seems elephants can't stand the smell of camels. How you can care for your newly acquired and treasured pet camel is another problem, but at least those elephants won't come around anymore.

People are a bit like elephants in their reactions, except they are far less fussy. They will retreat at any smell from another human, holding their breath and thinking BO. Our culture seems to tend towards eliminating smells rather than teaching their enjoyment. Any body odor is already considered evil. To be acceptable to members of the opposite sex one had best smell like a flower, hospital, lemon, or almost anything other than a body.

The sense of smell is actually one of the most powerful and primitive senses man has. Many primitive societies rely on the services of skilled sniffers to arrange compatible marriages. In fact, in nonliterate cultures the appearances of men and women are not taken as seriously as their odors.

Some scientists have claimed that man's sense of smell easily matches that of a hunting dog. Professional wine sniffers can tell by the bouquet the type of grape, where it was grown, and even the vineyard and vintage year. Perfume mixers can often detect mixed essences as small as one part in millions. An average person can detect two thousand different odors but can double his capacity with a little training.

Perhaps such a highly developed sense of smell is the norm, while our relative lack of sensitive sniffers might be the unfortunate exception. In a culture where the very young are taught that so many smells are "bad" it becomes safer to grow up not being able to smell too keenly. Many pleasurable smells come from nature and are rarely experienced in the city; others come from people, and we've learned to consider them unpleasant. So why smell at all?

Some sort of olfactory education is needed to retrain the sense of smell as a greater source of enjoyment, to reexamine which smells are genuinely unpleasant to humans and which are learned, and to enlarge the capacity to enjoy smells.

Smell Exercises

Discuss what the group knows about smell; how people learn to label smells pleasant or unpleasant.

Share the most memorable smell experience of your life. What is the earliest smell you can remember?

Have students be aware of smells on a walk around the school, the room, or the school grounds.

Bring various smells to class in such a way that they cannot be identified by sight. This can be done by placing each smell in a bag (brown paper bags usually have their own smell and should be avoided) or by simply having everyone close his eyes. Pass the smells around, and have each person experience the odor and then tell what it reminds him of. Smells have a power to evoke past experiences, often back to early childhood. The person could either tell of a past experience the smell recalls or fantasize from the smell. Greater group involvement can be gained if each person is responsible for bringing one or more smells. In this experience the emphasis should be on experiencing the smell and not on identifying odors. After the exercise there will be discussion on what the smells were, but the experience should not be turned into an identification contest.

An experiment using the sense of smell can be tried to demonstrate the fact that no sense is purely biological. Convince the class that you have a bottle containing a liquid known as "peppermint concentrate," an extremely powerful smell candy makers use to flavor peppermint. Place the bottle equidistant from everyone and explain that the experiment is to test who is most sensitive to smells and will detect the odor from the bottle first. A short explanation of how odors diffuse through the air with a few scientific-sounding terms such as diffusion rate should convince the group you are serious. The liquid should actually be water with food coloring added to convince the skeptics.

Hopefully, a number of people will shortly claim they smell the faint peppermint smell. Have the group close their eyes (to concentrate better on the smell, tell them) and hold up a hand and open the eyes only when the smell is noticed. See how many bite.

The demonstration is of a process known as "setting." Stated simply it means that the effect of something is largely dependent on expectations. A marijuana user who sincerely believes pot causes psychotic reactions might very likely have such reactions simply because he expects them. The experiment could also serve to introduce the concept of psychosomatic illness or even prejudice.

More Sense Exercises
Some suggestions for sense-awareness exercises to try outside of a school or group situation:

Try eating without utensils.

If you usually shower, take a bubble bath; if you normally bathe, try a shower. If used to a hot shower, try a cold one.

Find some habits in your diet or daily routine, and change them.

Go without meat for a week. Skip a meal. Try organic food.

Sleep on the floor or in a different room.

Go for a walk or ride at 5 A.M.

Ride a bike.

Smell flowers.

On your way home make a special effort to be sensually aware of the environment. Concentrate first on smell, then on sight, hearing, and touch.

Eat some food very slowly.

Try some food you don't like but haven't tried for years.

Fully enjoy falling asleep and waking up.

Enjoy stretching.

Spend time listening to music without doing anything else.

If you never dance, try dancing alone, at home.

Try a water bed.

Climb a tree.

Enjoy being naked.

Take a walk in the rain or snow.

Eat something you've never eaten before.

If you don't cook, learn.

Try ethnic restaurants.

Order the most unusual item at a restaurant.

Make one change in your clothing to be more comfortable.

Bake some bread.

Spend a night only with candlelight or with no light.

Learn a new skill—play a recorder; learn darts; ski; learn needlework or knitting or macrame or golf or tennis.

Go for a ride or walk in a ghetto you don't visit often—either urban or suburban.

Attend a church service of some religion about which you know little.

Wear something outrageous.

BACKGROUND READING: SENSE EDUCATION

The Adjusted American: Normal Neurosis in the Individual and Society by Snell and Gail Putney (New York: Harper & Row, 1964). Anyone who is normal has to be neurotic is the theme of this provocative work originally published in hardcover as *Normal Neurosis.* The authors state that many marriages are miserable because people marry for love, that the "adjusted American" becomes normal at the expense of his own humanity, that conformity deals with the unquestioned assumptions of our culture. These are only three of the challenges to what is accepted as truth that the book offers in a readable style. Chapters are on conformity, hatred and prejudice, self-acceptance, social isolation, sexualization, intimacy, parental love and obligation.

The Angry Book by Theodore Isaac Rubin, M.D. (New York: Macmillan, 1969) is an easy-to-read essay encouraging readers to allow themselves to be constructively angry. He blames many psychological problems on people's inability to feel and express anger. Feelings of anger that are unexpressed are converted into what Rubin calls a "slush fund" and manifest themselves in perverted ways ranging from overeating to sadism. The 200-page paperback also includes a 100-question self-examination on anger.

Big Rock Candy Mountain is the *Whole Earth Catalog* of the educational world. It is aimed especially at those in the free-school movement and those who wish to educate themselves outside of schools. The catalog is one hundred oversized pages of book reviews, classroom materials, process learning, home learning, and self-discovery. It is published six times yearly with two large issues in June and December and four smaller issues during the year. Subscriptions are $8 from Portola Institute Inc., 1115 Merrill St., Menlo Park, Calif. 94025.

The Betrayal of the Body by Alexander Lowen, M.D. (New York: Collier, 1969) describes and theorizes about schizophrenia in a technical manner that was never intended for a general audience. The book did catch on and was well received in paperback. Dr. Lowen states that a feeling of identity stems from a feeling of contact with one's body and that society discourages individuals from being "in touch" with their bodies. Society therefore unwittingly encourages schizoid tendencies and considers them normal. Difficult reading for high school students without a background in the vocabulary of psychology.

Body Language by Julius Fast (New York: M. Evans & Co., 1970) is a best-selling and entertaining survey of proxemics, kinesics, and nonverbal communication. The book reads easily and requires no special knowledge of psychology. Chapter titles include "The Body is the Message," "How We Handle Space," "The Masks Men Wear," "The Wonderful World of Touch," "An Alphabet for Movement," and others.

Education and Ecstacy by George B. Leonard (New York: Dell, 1969) outlines the goals for the schools of the future as follows: (1) to learn the commonly agreed upon skills and knowledge of the culture and to learn it joyfully and to learn that it is all tentative, (2) to learn how to bring creative change on all that is currently agreed upon, (3) to learn delight rather than aggression, cooperation instead of competition, sharing instead of acquisition, and uniqueness instead of conformity, (4) to learn heightened awareness and control of emotions, sense, and bodily states and thereby empathy for others, (5) to learn how to enter and enjoy varying states of consciousness, (6) to learn to explore and enjoy the infinite possibilities in relations between people, and (7) to learn how to learn. An excellent and widely read book.

The Greening of America by Charles A. Reich (New York: Random House, 1970) is another bestseller that tries to explain and point out the delights of a change in consciousness. Enough has already been written about the book to make further details here unnecessary except to suggest that it could be used on an assignment or required reading basis in paperback.

I'm OK–You're OK: A Practical Guide to Transactional Analysis by Thomas A. Harris, M.D. (New York: Harper & Row, 1969). Eric Berne popularized transactional analysis with his best selling *Games People Play*, but Thomas Harris does a much better job of explaining what it's all about. A teacher familiar with the concepts of TA gained from *I'm OK–You're OK* can use the language and concepts for group work in the classroom.

Improvisation for the Theater by Viola Spolin (Evanston: Northwestern University Press, 1963) is a 400-page hardcover that sells for around $9. Viola Spolin's theater-game techniques have spawned local theaters sponsoring improvisational theater-game nights for those who want their entertainment as participants instead of as spectators. The book describes about 200 games that have been played with children and teens learning to act, games that involve emotional expression, sensory awareness, a sense of place, etc. The ideas are easily adaptable to personal-relations work and are fun.

The Intelligent Eye by R. Gregory (New York: McGraw-Hill, 1970) contains a fascinating array of optical illusions and "impossible pictures." Try a public library for this one.

Joy: Expanding Human Awareness by William C. Schutz (New York: Grove, 1967) explains some of the ideas and techniques used at places like the Esalen Institute in Big Sur, California. The book is designed to help people truly feel again. Dr. Schutz states that, for many people, tension has become such a normal state that they are unaware they are tense at all. An excellent introduction to the theory behind sensitivity training. In his second book *Here Comes Everybody* (New York: Harcourt, Brace, Jovanovich, 1971), Schutz goes into more detail of the techniques used by encounter groups.

Mannerisms of Speech and Gestures in Everyday Life by Sandor S. Feldman (New York: International Universities Press, 1969) is a Freudian analysis of slips of the tongue, speech patterns, and gestures. He analyzes over 120 speech mannerisms from "It's not my business, but . . ." to "Let Me Make one thing perfectly clear," and digs into their real and hidden meanings. In spite of its almost total dependence on Freudian concepts the book has many insights into very ordinary behavior and makes fascinating reading. It is arranged with one- or two-page sections devoted to each gesture or mannerism, allowing students to look up the expressions they use—or even the ones the teacher uses.

The Pleasure Seekers: The Drug Crisis, Youth and Society by Joel Fort, M.D. (New York: Bobbs-Merrill, 1969) is among the best books on drugs available. Dr. Fort is well aware of the myths being generated about drugs and backs his minority-position views with extensive research and a questioning mind. Available in paperback.

Self-Awareness Through Group Dynamics by Richard Reichert (Dayton, Ohio: Pflaum, 1970) is a $1.95 paperback aimed at high school teachers. The most valuable parts of the book are the practical teaching suggestions for "do-it-yourself" simulations on about a dozen different topics. Any high school teacher should be able to get at least one or two good ideas from the game suggestions, making the book a worthwhile investment.

Sense Relaxation by Bernard Gunther (New York: Collier Books, 1968) is a must for teaching about the senses. The large $3.50 paperback, subtitled "A Book of Experiments in Being Alive," gives exercises for individuals, partners, and groups to achieve greater sensory awareness. Many of the exercises are adaptable to class or group use.

The Silent Language by Edward T. Hall (New York: Doubleday, 1959) is probably the first book about body language that gained popularity. The book (available in paperback) explores how time and space are conceived and used differently in different cultures. Anthropological in approach, the book makes excellent background reading. *The Hidden Dimension* is another book by Edward Hall that also concerns body language.

Structured Experiences for Human Relations Training by J. William Pfeiffer and John E. Jones (Iowa City, Iowa: University Associates Press, 1969-71) is so far a work of three volumes each selling for $3. Each volume contains detailed descriptions of about 25 "structured experiences" often similar to those described in the first part of this book. Some of the experiences are for industry and business, others for encounter group leaders, but many are easily adaptable to the general classroom. An excellent series of books available from University Associates Press, P.O. Box 615, Iowa City, Iowa 52240.

Total Loss Farm by Raymond Mungo (New York: E. P. Dutton,

1970) is a personal narrative in the tradition of *On the Road* and *The Strawberry Statement*. Raymond Mungo is definitely Consciousness III, if not IV, and a sensitive artist as well. For example, he speaks of preservatives added to food to keep them fresh: "The sole advantage of preservatives to the consumer, it seems, is that he can now save money by buying day-old or month-old baked goods and be certain that they will taste like cold putty no matter their birthday." *Total Loss Farm* is the diary of a man in touch with his senses.

Understanding Drug Use: An Adult's Guide to Drugs and the Young by Peter Marin and Allan Cohen (New York: Harper & Row, 1971) should be required reading for teachers and parents. Let the authors speak for themselves here: "Adults who worry about their children must finally understand that our institutions do not help them and usually do them harm. There is no one to help but ourselves, and the task that confronts us is an unfamiliar one: not how to adjust them to things, but how to find them viable alternatives, how to liberate the young from everything designed to do them 'good.'"

RELATED AREAS TO STUDY IN A UNIT OR COURSE ON SENSE EDUCATION

Optical illusions
Sense overload—hypnotism
Sense deprivation—hallucinations
Noise pollution
Sleep and dreams
Body language
ESP
The occult
Insanity
Obscenity, pornography
Personal relations in other cultures
Zen
Drugs (To make a unit on drugs part of the whole unit on sense education would make more sense than to isolate drugs as a special study.)
Various schools of psychology—Gestalt, Reality Therapy, Transactional Analysis, Logotherapy
The invention of adolescence
Freedom-repression

Suicide
Alternative life-styles—communes, dropouts, hippies, subcultures

FILMS

Anastenaria

Anastenaria was made as an anthropological study of Dionysian elements in modern Greek rituals but is fascinating to any audience above the grade school level. The Anastenaria is a form of popular worship, still practiced in some sections of Greece, which involves a fire-walking ritual. The feast occurs on May 21, the Greek Orthodox Holy Day of St. Constantine and his mother St. Helen. Scientists are unable to explain how the villagers dance, even stomp, on the burning embers without pain or harm to their bare feet. The fire walking climaxes the ritual, which also includes a ceremonial slaughter of an unblemished animal who has lived an odd number of years, the distribution of the animal to the village, the use of holy water as protection, icons, ecstatic dancing, incense, and healing.

The film documents the ritual objectively and without frills. The ritual provides a glimpse at the potential of man to adapt and overcome even pain. The film is excellent for a discussion of human potential, ecstacy, other cultures, religion, ritual, or simply as a mind-expanding experience for the skeptical.

(17 min., b&w, 1967, UC) See Appendix I for key to film sources.

Art and Perception, Learning to See

This teaching film is an introduction to the development of visual awareness. The film proposes that a creative visual response to the environment depends on a sharp observant eye and an imaginative way of expressing what is seen. The film encourages students to focus on the elements of color, line, pattern, texture, shapes, light and shadow in scenes of the country, city, and seashore. Juxtaposing scenes of farmyards, streets, and beaches with paintings allows students to understand how various artists of many eras have perceived and reacted to the objects, mood, and atmosphere of life around them. Aimed at art classes, but interesting enough for general appeal.

(17 min., color, 1970, BFA)

ESP: The Human "X" Factor
Originally shown on National Educational Television, this program investigates the world of ESP at Duke University's Parapsychology Laboratory. Electronic cameras recorded subjects tested for clairvoyance, telepathy, precognition and psychokinesis. Dr. J. B. Rhine discusses his attempts to prove the existence of ESP and its possible relationship with psychosomatic ailments and religion.
(30 min., b&w, 1967, PSU)

The Evolution of a Yogi
According to Buddha, "man's problem is his attachment to thoughts and senses" which binds him to illusion and creates suffering. This is how Baba Ram Dass, alias Richard Alpert, Ph.D., introduces viewers to the Hindu method of Yoga.

The Yoga technique is to utilize each of the senses with dispassion and yet full involvement. Westerners talk while they eat or think of things other than the food at hand. This results not only in a lessened enjoyment of the food but also in a tendency to eat much more than is really needed. The Yogi is one who can extricate himself from his thoughts and senses.

Thought processes are also seen as hindrances to attaining unity. Meditation is used to shut down the constant stream of thoughts that clutter the mind.

Ram Dass is shown teaching the way of Yoga to others using body positions, breath control, meditation before a candle flame, singing, and dancing. All these techniques are aimed at banishing the distinction between subject and object to attain pure consciousness.
(28 min., color, Hartley Productions)

The Eye of the Beholder
Few teaching films made as long ago as 1955 remain relevant today. *The Eye of the Beholder* is one of the few exceptions. The film dramatizes the story of 12 hours in the life of Michael Gerard, an artist. After a brief introduction which makes the point that we can easily be misled, we see Michael in his studio, standing amid a disarray of spilled paints and a knife, with an apparently lifeless young woman lying on a couch.

From here the film flashes back to give the impressions Michael has made in the minds of five people. These five describe him as a good boy, a hood, a lady's man, a loony, and a murderer. The viewer doesn't know what Michael Gerard is.

In the second half of the film Michael himself is interviewed, and we get his point of view. Like the others, he is partly right and partly wrong.

The film is excellent for discussion; a study guide should accompany it when ordered.

(25 min., b&w, FSU, KSU, MMM, MSU, NYU, SUNYB, UC, UIll, UInd, UM, UMn, USF)

Flatland

Flatland is only indirectly about the senses. It was originally intended as a mathematical parable, based on a book written in the nineteenth century by Edwin Abbot.

Flatland is an imaginary two-dimensional world inhabited by squares, triangles, and octagons. The society based status and occupation on shape. In this 2-D world a little square naturally explained the world as two-dimensional: there was no such thing as up or down in a 2-D world, only north and south. The little square was inquisitive, but his basic questions were brushed aside.

One day a visitor from the third dimension, a wonderful sphere, visited the little square and took him to see the third dimension. The junior nonconformist returned to Flatland with a radically changed world view. He tried to explain the wonders of the third dimension to the wise elders but, of course, was unsuccessful, since one cannot possibly explain the third dimension to people who believe there are only two. He failed and was placed in jail for heresy or the 2-D version of radicalism.

The new experiences and frustrations of the little square make this a relevant film for anyone attempting to see in new ways.

(12 min., color, animated, CF, UM)

Invisible Walls

Invisible Walls is about the wall eighteen inches from our bodies in which we Americans mentally encase ourselves. The space inside of this invisible wall we unconsciously guard as personal. The film records a candid-camera sort of experiment in which pedestrians were stopped for an interview only to have their personal space violated. Strangers who invade this 18 inches of personal space are told in body language to back off or their closeness is considered an attack. Such behavior is learned, the narrator points out, and is different from culture to culture. Americans are physically aloof compared to other cultures who also live in crowded cities. American children accept contact as a part of life but soon learn to restrict touching to a highly limited set of conditions. The film concludes that with increases in city size and population we either have to learn to tolerate more invasions of our personal space or learn to enjoy physical closeness.

The film is excellent for discussion and provides a fine introduction to the topic of body language.

(12 min., b&w, UC, PSU)

Kevin

Kevin is a young boy of about ten who is blind. The film shows how his experiences of the world differ from that of the sighted by having the boy talk about the things he touches, hears and smells. "I like to touch the grass . . . I can tell what color it is by touching it" and "I like thunder . . . at night it breaks the dead silence that's around" are examples of Kevin's special way of perceiving his environment.

All of the gentle, poetic thoughts that come from Kevin are matched with equally sensitive cinematography that captures the boy in his favorite position in life, alone in the midst of nature. Although Kevin has never seen the trees, sky, and sun shown on the screen, it becomes evident that he nevertheless has a supranormal ability to sense and describe the world around him.

(20 min., b&w, Churchill, Pyramid, PSU, UM)

The Searching Eye

The Searching Eye is a Saul Bass (*Why Man Creates*) production that resembles a long Kodak commercial. Its sentiments are lofty and mood contemplative. The film has won many film awards from Venice to Chicago in spite of its script, which is little more than a collection of lofty clichés.

The vehicle for meditation on sight and insight is an afternoon in the life of a ten-year-old boy. The lad goes to a beach and plays; he looks and sees. The excellent film visuals show what he sees and the world he cannot see. The film is valuable for its beautiful photography and for the awareness it does create about the world around us that remains unseen.

(18 min., color, 1968, Pyramid, UC, UM)

Silent Snow, Secret Snow
Silent Snow, Secret Snow is an adaption of the Conrad Aiken short story about Paul, a young boy who gradually withdraws from the real world to live completely within his frighteningly private but wonderful world of the silent, secret snow that he alone sees on his own street.

Paul's teacher and parents become worried at his withdrawal, but Paul will not share his incommunicable and secret world with them. His secret gives him a wall to hide behind, a screen of new snow between himself and the world. As a doctor and Paul's parents question him about his withdrawn behavior he tells them he is "thinking about the snow—that's all." He runs from the "inquisition" up to his room and finds it filled with snow, drifting comfortingly over everything. In a final act of personal excommunication from reality he rebukes his mother and falls asleep in his imaginary snow, listening intently as the snow voices tell him their own story.

The Aiken short story is a writer's description of schizophrenia, although the universality of the creation of dream worlds makes the film a discussion aid to the world of shared personal and private awarenesses.

(17 min., b&w, AB)

To See or Not to See
This short animation from the National Film Board of Canada shows a doctor and patient conducting a scientific inquiry into the merit of illusion.

The evolution of the patient's attitudes toward the world (called his psyche) is sketched using a cartoon figure similar to Casper the Ghost; the image represents the patient's mental and emotional activity. Through childhood and early adulthood the patient's psyche lives in ease; reality is made to conform to the demands of fantasy and illusion. Recently, however, reality has been gaining strength through a series of disasters that produce acute anxiety. Having tried drugs and alcohol to no avail, the patient submits to the doctor's treatment—special "glasses."

Thrust out into the world for the test, the patient is run over by a steamroller whose potential danger the glasses had minimized. The optimistic doctor failed to cure his patient.

Should we strive to see things as they really are and let reality crush us, or should we don the glasses of illusion and unreality and be bowled over by lack of perception of reality? That is the question: to see or not to see.

(15 min., color, animated, LCA)

FILMS TO SEE, TASTE, AND TOUCH

The films which follow are cinematic studies of objects or activities which normally escape awareness. The films are without narration and many involve extreme close-ups or slow motion to help the viewer observe what he had previously only seen.

Allures

Jordan Belson worked for a year and a half in his basement piecing together this film, which is intended to carry the viewer from the outer to the inner self, from matter to spirit. As Belson says, "I think of *Allures* as a combination of molecular structures and astronomical events mixed up with subconscious and subjective phenomena—all happening simultaneously. The beginning is almost purely sensual, the end perhaps totally non-material."

(9 min., color, Pyramid)

The Big Shave

A bloody, gory close-up of a man calmly shaving himself to death. Produces strong feelings in the audience, often of repulsion.

(6 min., color, CF, UC, Pyramid)

Bread

A Charles Eames study in the texture of a food that has all been replaced in our culture with packaged air and plastic that helps deceive mothers eight ways.

(6 min., color, 1953, USC)

Corral

A sensitive study of the roping and riding of a high-spirited horse.

(12 min., b&w, CF, Pyramid, CFS, PSU, ROA, UU, UC)

Corrida Interdite
By Denys Colomb de Daunant, who also made the popular *Dream of Wild Horses*. Majestic slow motion of the struggle between man and bull. Organ music as soundtrack helps give the impression of bullfight as a form of ritual.
(10 min., color, Pyramid, CFS)

Dream of Wild Horses
Slow motion and soft-focus backgrounds create dreamlike effects in the motion of wild horses.
(9 min., color, CF, KSU, CU, Pyramid, PSU, UC, CFS)

Dunes
Fred Hudson has a feel for nature and is able to capture that feeling in his sensitive nature studies.
(7 min., color, Pyramid, UIll)

Ecology—Checks and Balances
Amazing microphotography of the life struggle between aphids and ladybugs. This film is narrated.
(14 min., color, Pyramid)

Embryo
Pheasants are shown at mating time fighting for the right to mate with the female. The egg develops and is shown through time-lapse photography.
(10 min., color, Pyramid)

Junkyard
There is much beauty to be found in as unlikely a place as a junkyard, especially as the seasons change.
(10 min., color, BFA)

Leaf
A Fred Hudson film. The odyssey of an autumn leaf.
(7 min., color, Pyramid)

Moods of Surfing
A mean film to show in Kansas in midwinter. Nonnarrated study of the joys and dangers of surfing.
(15 min., color, Pyramid)

Necrology
One continuous shot of the faces of a 5:00 P.M. crowd descending via the Pan Am building escalators. A subtle sort of power.
(12 min., b&w, CCC)

Omega
Donald Fox's award-winning optical poem. A dash of *Space Odyssey,* a bit of Chardin, and wall-to-wall special effects make *Omega* a meditation on the destiny of man.
(13 min., color, Pyramid)

Overture/Nyitany
A chick hatches complete with Beethoven overture.
(15 min., color, CF)

Rodeo
One of the most tactile short films around. Cowboy and rodeo in super slow motion and hand-held camera.
(20 min., color, CF)

Ski the Outer Limits
Some excellent slow motion and lab effects of skiers. The narrator gets carried away and sounds best with the volume off—make up your own music.
(29 min., color, Pyramid, NU)

Skin
Sex, skin, and sensuality as a part of nature and beauty. Many superimposed images and rather startling editing give the film a rich texture and deep tactility. Not for classes where the body must be covered to be seen.
(12 min., color, CCC)

Sky
A National Film Board of Canada study of the changing moods of the sky in one day.
(10 min., color, CF, KSU, Pyramid)

Winter Geyser
Another fine Fred Hudson nature film.
(7 min., color, Pyramid)

IDDEN ASSUMPTIONS

The most important thing . . . we can know about a man is what he takes for granted, and the most elemental and important facts about a society are those that are seldom debated and generally regarded as "settled."

Louis Wirth

The failure of the American school system is a sign of hope; its success would be a disaster. In any culture the purpose of schooling is to adapt the human potential to the existing culture, not to develop that potential. If a culture values skill in headhunting or cannibalism the school system can be considered successful if it trains students to be crafty headhunters and cannibals. An outsider with Western morals who would enter such a society as a critic and blame the schools for the problem of headhunting would be guilty of a gross failure to understand the culture. So it is with our schools.

Jules Henry in *Culture Against Man* puts it nicely:

The function of education has never been to free the mind and the spirit of man, but to bind them; and to the end that the mind and spirit of his children should never escape homo sapiens has employed praise, ridicule, admonition, accusation, mutilation and even torture to chain them to the culture pattern. Throughout most of his historic course homo sapiens has wanted from his children acquiescence, not originality. It is natural that this should be so, for where every man is unique there is no society, and where there is no society there can be no man. . . . It stands to reason that were young people truly creative the culture would fall apart, for originality, by definition, is different from what is given, and what is given is culture itself.

If our schools are "grim, joyless places" as Charles Silberman discovered, it is not because they are run by "mindless" men (it would seem safe to say that if there are mindless men they are nicely distributed among the various fields of human enterprise) but because society depends on joylessness to conduct its daily business effectively. If our schools are based on fear, as John Holt says, it is because we believe fear keeps our society stable. If they induce alienation, as Paul Goodman observes, it is because our society could not exist as it is without masses of alienated individuals. If they punish creativity and independence, as Edgar Friedenberg claims, it is simply because creativity and independence are not valued as qualities which preserve the culture.

So most proponents of "radical school reform" are really social reformists hoping to achieve this reform through the schools. These critics know that schools exist to preserve the status quo and hope they can change the schools from agents of preservation to catalysts of change. They hope that schools will help students see the insanity of many national values considered "normal." They would like to see educational systems which foster human potential, freedom, creativity, and independence.

Until the Messiah of sweeping educational revolution comes, teachers in high school will be faced with a recurring problem—students who have been subject to at least eight years of institutional training and at least fourteen years of parental instruction. Some of this instruction will have been a benefit to the students' survival, but much of it will have served to limit his potential severely. The teaching suggestions which follow are designed to help students realize their own prejudices, hidden assumptions, cultural taken-for-granteds, and learned values. Once realized, the values can be freely chosen or replaced by more appropriate ones.

The activities and discussions involved could possibly be used as a "unit" in traditional subject areas such as the social sciences or the language arts. It would fit nicely into courses offered in some schools on other cultures, anthropology, psychology, the condition of man, or religion. The ideas could be integrated into studies of novels, communication, American problems, or even history. If the division of "subject matter" into departments makes the ideas which follow difficult to classify, then those divisions ought to be very critically examined.

The ideas given here ought to be adapted to local situations rather than followed exactly as described.

A TEST FOR HIDDEN ASSUMPTIONS

The most effective way to detect hidden assumptions is to catch yourself in the act of making the assumption. This is particularly true if by making the assumption you run into a brick wall of sorts. The little boy in the house of mirrors catches himself making a hidden and painfully false assumption when he walks through an open doorway only to find it's really clear glass. The following test is designed to reveal hidden assumptions which prevent the solution of rather simple problems.

Give each person a copy of this test (it may be reproduced for classroom use only without permission), and allow about twenty minutes for completion. Most students will correctly answer only a few questions at most, and rare will be the individual who scores the traditional passing grade of 70 percent.

After the test is taken, correct it in class, and discuss the reasons for the many wrong answers. Students will often react at first by saying they were tricked, but this still doesn't answer the question. Point out that there was no complicated mathematics or technical knowledge required to pass the test. Sharp ten-year-olds will score as well as high school seniors and adults, often much higher.

Each question involves a hidden assumption. For example, in question number one the reader assumes the two men are playing each other, although such an assumption is not warranted by the facts. Question two traps people who have taken many tests before in the assumption that correct information is always provided in test questions. Question seven is an example of past experience acting to limit creativity; corks are for removing and not for pushing into bottles.

Each question should be discussed briefly before considering the more general implications of the entire test. Possible discussion question would include: Why did you have so many wrong answers? What misleading assumptions did you make in answering each question? Why were those assumptions made? Would a college professor be likely to score well on this test? Is this test in any way a valid test of learning or education? Do such hidden assumptions take place in more significant areas of life? What are some hidden assumptions which prevent entire cultures from solving crucial problems?

A Test

1. Two men played chess. They played five games, and each man won three. How do you explain this? _____

2. Answer this question within five seconds and do not return to check your answer: How many animals of each species did Adam take aboard the Ark with him? (Note—the question is *not* how many pairs, but how many animals.) _____

3. An archaeologist reported that he had discovered two gold coins in the desert near Jerusalem dated 439 B.C. Many of his fellow scientists refused to take his claim seriously. Why? _____

4. If you had only one match and you entered a room to start a kerosene lamp, an oil heater, and a wood-burning stove, which would you light first and why? _____

5. Here is a question on international law: if an *international* airliner crashed exactly on the U.S.-Mexican border, where would they be required by law to bury the survivors? (Do not spend more than ten seconds on this question) _____

6. You have four nines (9, 9, 9, 9). Arrange them to total 100. You may use any of the arithmetical processes (addition, subtraction, multiplication, or division). Each nine must be used once and only once. _____

7. You have a dime in an empty wine bottle. The bottle is corked. Your job is to get the dime out of the bottle without taking the cork out. You must do this without damaging the bottle in any way. How would you do it? _____

8. Explain the following true boast: "In my bedroom, the nearest lamp that I usually keep turned on is 12 feet away from my bed. Alone in the room, without using wires, strings, or any other aids or contraptions, I can turn out the light on that lamp and get into bed before the room is dark." _____

9. Draw four straight lines through all nine dots without lifting pen or pencil from the paper:

   •   •   •

   •   •   •

   •   •   •

10. Memorize the phrases below. As soon as you do that turn the paper over and write them at the top of the back of this page. Do not look back at the phrases once you have turned this page over.

PARIS	ONCE
IN THE	IN A
THE SPRING	A LIFETIME
BIRD	SLOW
IN THE	MEN AT
THE HAND	AT WORK

Answers to: *A Test*

1. They didn't play the games with each other.
2. Adam didn't go on an ark. Noah did.
3. The date B.C. couldn't have been used before Christ.
4. The match.
5. Survivors aren't buried.
6. $99 + 9 \div 9 = 100$ or $99 + \frac{9}{9} = 100$
7. Push the cork in the bottle and shake the dime out.
8. He does it in the daytime.
9.

10. Note that each phrase has a repeated word.

DETECTING STEREOTYPES

Redheads have hot tempers; Swedes all have blond hair; blacks are super-athletes; Mexicans are lazy; and women are less rational than men. These are a few of the falsehoods or half-truths that form part of our common stereotypes. Those who believe them are generally unaware that their opinions constitute stereotypes. They usually believe that such opinions are based on observation and statistics; in short, common sense. The following test is designed to detect and help define stereotypes held by class members. The test will not challenge the validity of the stereotype, only point out its existence.

Half the group participating in the questionnaire-test receives version number one, and the other half version number two. This could be done within each class or with a number of classes. The existence of two versions of the questionnaire should not be known. The questionnaire is titled "Evaluating People on Incomplete Information," in order to satisfy those who will claim they really can't decide and also to avoid preconceptions about stereotypes.

Each of the five people in the questionnaire has one quality different in the two versions. In item number one, for example, the only difference between the two Janes is hair color. It would seem safe to say that if the easygoing–hot-tempered scale receives a higher total of choice for the red-haired Jane, then the stereotype that "redheads are hotheads" exists among the group. Item number two evaluates the Latin American stereotype, number three the Negro, number four the female, and number five the adolescent.

After the questionnaire, tally the results for each item and discuss with the class the idea of stereotypes. Discussion and research could concern the validity of the stereotype, the existence of other stereotypes not touched upon in the questionnaire, the effect of stereotyping upon both the person who holds the stereotype and the person to whom it is applied.

Evaluating People on Incomplete Information
Instructions: Below are descriptions of five different people. From the bit of information given circle the number which best indicates what sort of person each of the five is.
1. Jane is 21 years old and a senior in college. She is 5′2″ tall and has red hair. She makes average grades and dates about twice a week. She probably is:

Intelligent	1	2	3	4	5 Stupid
Easygoing	1	2	3	4	5 Hot-tempered
Conservative	1	2	3	4	5 Liberal
Attractive	1	2	3	4	5 Unattractive

2. George Rodriguez is 34 years old, is employed at a department store, is married, and has six children. He probably is:

Friendly	1	2	3	4	5 Unfriendly
Intelligent	1	2	3	4	5 Stupid
Good public speaker	1	2	3	4	5 Poor public speaker
Steady	1	2	3	4	5 Temperamental
Ambitious	1	2	3	4	5 Lazy

3. Frank Burton is 32, black, married to a high school graduate, and works at a restaurant. He probably is:

Friendly	1	2	3	4	5 Unfriendly
Intelligent	1	2	3	4	5 Stupid
Ambitious	1	2	3	4	5 Lazy
Happy-go-Lucky	1	2	3	4	5 Serious

4. Joan works at Bell Telephone Company, is married, and has one child. She probably is:

Competent	1	2	3	4	5	Incompetent
Content	1	2	3	4	5	Discontent
Rational	1	2	3	4	5	Emotional
Artistic	1	2	3	4	5	Scientific

5. James is a 16-year-old high school student in a suburban school. He works in the summer for a local newspaper, dates most every weekend, and enjoys automobiles. He probably is:

Intelligent	1	2	3	4	5	Stupid
Polite	1	2	3	4	5	Rude
Law-abiding	1	2	3	4	5	Lawbreaker
Nice guy	1	2	3	4	5	Bad guy

Version two of the questionnaire is identical to the one above except that each of the descriptions should be changed as follows:

1. Jane is 21 years old and a senior in college. She is 5'2" tall and has brown hair. She makes average grades and dates about twice a week. She probably is:

2. James Winthrop is 34 years old, is employed at a department store, is married, and has six children. He probably is:

3. Frank Burton is 32 years old, married to a high school graduate, and works at a restaurant. He probably is:

4. John works at Bell Telephone Company, is married, and has one child. He probably is:

5. James is a 26-year-old high school teacher in a suburban school. He

works in the summer for a local newspaper, dates almost every weekend, and enjoys automobiles. He probably is:

THE COMPETITION ASSUMPTION
The simulation game described here is one in which success will be proportionate to the ability of the group to cooperate with each other rather than to compete. Because our culture values competition and teaches it in school most people when put in a game situation (or any situation) will try to "beat" the other guy (or defend themselves). This game makes that hidden assumption clear and raises questions about its value.

The game works with groups of eight. After ten rounds of "Score as Much as Possible," the final scores are totaled for the group or groups and invariably the group will have fallen together, having failed to "score as much as possible." Group members are not told that they are to compete with each other, nor are they told to co-operate; they are left to assume which is correct. Rarely is the assumption even questioned; competition is quickly assumed to be the proper stance.

After the game, analyze why the competition assumption was made and how it influenced the final score. Discuss how this assumption affects our society in both entertainment and business. Envision how a society would be different if people made a cooperation assumption instead of a competition assumption. Discuss a grading system for a class that would give the entire class the lowest grade scored by any one of its members. Invent a game which would still be fun but would be based on cooperation instead of competition.

Rules for "Score as Much as Possible"
For the game the group should be divided into groups of eight and positioned in movable desks, chairs, or seated on the floor like this:

$$\begin{matrix} & \circ\ \circ & \\ \circ & & \circ \\ \circ & & \circ \\ & \circ\ \circ & \end{matrix}$$

There can be many groups of eight in one room if necessary. Each group operates independently of the others: there is no competition or cooperation between groups. Within each group are four sets of partners. If the group is not divisible exactly by eight, some can act as judges, score-keepers and time-keepers. After the people are grouped, give out the score sheet for the game, one to each set of partners (four to a group). Tell them to study the score sheet for about four minutes and try to figure out how to play the game. Be sure to mention the title of the game out loud.

After the four minutes, tell the groups the following rules:

1. You may confer only with your partner unless otherwise instructed (as they will be in rounds 5, 8, and 10). Secret signals are not allowed.

2. Each set of partners must agree on a single choice for each round—an X or a Y.

Begin playing the game. Each set of partners should fill in the score sheet as the game progresses. Sample scoring for a round: Let's say that in one group one set of partners chooses X and the other three choose Y. According to the score sheet, the partners that chose the X would win three points while the three sets of partners who chose Y would each lose one point. Note that on rounds 5, 8, and 10, group consultation is allowed and the scores are doubled, tripled, or quintupled. Conduct each round; keep time; inform the groups when they can consult and when choices must be made; make sure everyone is following the rules.

After round 10, each group of eight should figure out its total score. Here is the catch. The title of the game, "Score as Much as Possible" refers to the group as a whole and not to the partners. The idea of the game is for the group to score as many points as possible. If they all chose Y for each round, the group total would be plus 100. The group's success is judged by how close they came to a perfect game of plus 100. Many, if not most, groups will have scores below zero because of the assumption that competition was in order rather than cooperation.

After the final scoring, discuss what hidden assumptions the players made, why that assumption was made, how it hurt the total score, and in what other areas of life those same assumptions are made. Discuss any relationship between the game and the test given earlier. Discuss the group process during the game.

Score Sheet for "Score as Much as Possible"
Directions: For ten rounds you and your partner will choose either an
    X or a Y. The points scored in each round are dependent upon the

pattern of choice made by everyone in the group. Scoring will be according to the following:

4 Xs	Lose 1 point each
3 Xs 1 Y	Win 1 point each Lose 3 points
2 Xs 2 Ys	Win 2 points each Lose 2 points each
1 X 3 Ys	Win 3 points Lose 1 point each
4 Ys	Win 1 point each

Strategy: You can confer with your partner once each round and make a joint decision. Before rounds 5, 8, and 10 you can confer with the other members of the group.

Round	Time	Confer with	Choice	Points won	Points lost	
1	1 min.	partner				
2	30 sec.	partner				
3	30 sec.	partner				
4	30 sec.	partner				
5	2 min. 30 sec.	group partner				Bonus round double score
6	30 sec.	partner				
7	30 sec.	partner				
8	3 min. 30 sec.	group partner				Bonus round triple score
9	30 sec.	partner				
10	3 min. 30 sec.	group partner				Bonus round Multiply score by 5.
						TOTAL

There is a variation of this game which is far simpler to conduct but which does not involve the entire class. It makes the same point, however.

Choose two volunteers who have some spare change with them and are willing to make a little more. Explain that you have eight nickels which you will auction to them one at a time, highest bidder for each nickel getting that nickel. Allow no advice from the rest of the class. The two volunteers should alternate each time in making the first bid.

Keep track of each final bid for accounting purposes (you will likely lose a few pennies in this experiment). The more competitive the two volunteers the less you will lose. After the bidding discuss the results.

Point out that if the two had cooperated, each could have received sixteen cents—each purchasing four nickels for four cents if the first volunteer to bid each time bid one cent and the other refused to bid. Other discussion questions can be similar to those suggested for "Score as Much as Possible."

REVEALING AND EXAMINING VALUES

After the preceding experiences it should be evident to students that the factors which influence behavior are often hidden. The following exercise is designed to allow a group to reveal and examine values in a relatively low-threat situation. It also allows individuals to see the values of others very graphically and to compare them with their own. The "game" also requires literally "taking a stand" on value questions.

The game can be played with any number of people (even hundreds) but does require enough room for students to move around. A general rule is that the larger the group, the more superficial the examination of values will be. A series of statements are prepared to which students respond by placing themselves somewhere along a complete agreement-complete disagreement scale. Students actually take a physical stand rather than merely expressing an opinion on paper. One wall of the room represents complete agreement and the opposite wall represents complete disagreement. Along a side wall degrees of agreement and disagreement (agree somewhat, disagree somewhat) are marked off. Enough furniture should be cleared to make movement possible.

After each statement students take the position in the room that corresponds to their opinion. This is done with ten or more statements. For example, one statement might read: "A college student grows his hair long because everyone else is doing it." Students then move to the place in the room which best represents their approval or disapproval of such an action. The center of the room should be reserved for those who do not wish to express an opinion on the statement. The next statement could be: "A college student shaves his head bald just to be different." Students then move to a new position (or stay in the same position) and are asked to explain their move. The value judgment in this example concerns not long or short hair but the value of acting for peer approval.

The statements are paired in such a way that movement in a certain direction most often indicates a particular value (see chart which follows). In their book *Values and Teaching,* Louis Raths, Merrill Harmin, and Sidney Simon suggest an entire curriculum built on value education. A familiarity with their work is strongly suggested.

The following statements have been used successfully with high school students. Notice that in the following items there is an *A* and *B* or an *A, B* and *C* to each. The movement from *A* to *B* is meaningful, since *B* and *A* are identical except for a single change in the situation of one of the persons. The place a student chooses on any statement *A* is not as revealing as his movement after the reading of statement *B.* The items here are only suggestions and should be replaced with situations of current and local importance.

Disagree $\longleftrightarrow$ Agree

1. A. A high school student drives home from school without using his seat belt.
   B. A man with a wife and four children drives home from work without using a seat belt.

2. A. A high school senior (boy) tells a girl he will marry her. He does this only to get her to agree to sex. He does not intend to marry her.
   B. A high school senior (girl) tells a boy she will marry him. She does this only to get him to agree to sex. She does not intend to marry him.

3. A. A very attractive girl becomes a prostitute because she believes there is good money in it.
   B. A very attractive girl becomes a prostitute because she has to support her ill mother (no father) and five kids, and this is the only talent she has.

4. A. A teacher strikes a student who has called the teacher an obscene name.
   B. A student strikes a teacher who has called him an obscene name.

5. A. The school librarian cuts out pictures he believes to be dirty from books and magazines the library buys.
   B. The school librarian does not accept books which treat college radicals favorably.
   C. The school librarian does not accept books which strongly support the John Birch Society or other right-wing groups.

6. A. A businessman drinks two martinis every day for lunch.
   B. A businessman smokes two joints of marijuana every afternoon.
   C. The Surgeon General has just announced that marijuana is medically safe. The weed is still illegal. The businessman continues to smoke two joints every afternoon. (Movement should be based on businessman's activity only.)

7. A. A college student grows his hair long just because everyone else is doing it.
   B. A college student shaves his head bald just to be different.

8. A. A person who believes a war is immoral does not show up when drafted.
   B. A person who believes a war is just shows up when drafted and serves.
   C. A person who believes a war is immoral shows up for the draft and serves.

Those who move towards the disagree (left)
after statement B

> *Those who move towards the agree (right)*
> *after statement B*
>
> > *No movement*

Possibly indicates the recognition of a sense
of responsibility.

> > Often those who say seat belts are for "sissies."

Boys who move to the left from A to B
reveal the possible existence of the double
standard in their value system.

> Girls who move to the right after statement
> B reveal a value possibly based on acceptance
> of the double standard.

> > Respect or its complete lack but without in-
> > fluence from the double standard.

> Parental love or loyalty is probably valued
> more than the law or traditional sexual
> standards.

Shows value of respect for adult or school
authority.

> Values revenge, hostility, possibly justice
> more than respect for authority. Identifies
> more with antiauthority.

Any change of position from A to B or B to C indicates that the value
of freedom of information is subordinate or conditioned by its content.
Movement might indicate a readiness to accept forms of censorship.

Movement after statement B: values law over
    personal freedom or believes pot is more
    dangerous than alcohol.

Movement after statement C: probably does
    not approve of chemicals for mood
    changes.

Conformity to group standards.

> Values "being different" for its own sake more
> than conforming for its own sake.
> No movement after B often shows a person
> values following his conscience more than
> others.
>
>> After statement C: might show law valued
>> over conscience.

ASSUMPTIONS REFLECTED IN THE MIRROR OF LANGUAGE

To a careful listener most speech reveals more than the speaker in-
tends. Certain expressions and usages become part of a person's speech
mannerisms. These mannerisms are most often unexamined and often
reflect cultural bias. At other times mannerisms become linguistic cop-
outs, allowing a person to say one thing while meaning something
completely different. Following are some rather common mannerisms
and speech habits which, when examined, can lead to self and cultural
understanding. They are most effectively studied when they occur
normally in the course of the class.

Statements Disguised as Questions

A question mark is often a linguistic defense mechanism. Many "questions" are really statements of belief, feeling, or opinion masquerading
as questions. Phrasing a statement in question form allows the asker
to disown the opinion if the person questioned should belittle the
viewpoint. Those who fear revealing themselves publicly or who hesi-
tate to commit themselves will often end statements with question
marks.

Find an example in a group discussion of this tendency, and discuss it. There is no need to embarrass the person using this device,
since it is common to most people at some time.

For example, a student asks, "Why do we have to study history
again?" Chances are that 95 percent of such questions are simply
ways of saying "I feel studying history is stupid." The student does
not feel free enough to express his opinion directly and so makes his
statement in question form. What most often happens in such situations is the student receives an unwanted and unneeded lecture on
the value of history.

When such a "question" occurs in the course of discussion ask the person to rephrase it in terms of a statement about himself. A question like "Are we going to take a break during the class?" might finally come out "I want a drink of water."

I Can't

When a person uses the expression "I can't" he almost always means "I won't." A person can do almost anything, even fly. A person who wants to fly must be willing to pay the consequences of the fast stop at the bottom, however. If he is unwilling to pay this price, he is correct in saying "I won't fly," but not that "I can't." The word *can't*, even when placed before activities such as sing, dance, speak in public, or talk to strangers serves to place responsibility for the failure outside the person.

When a person uses "I can't" in this context have him say the same thing but change the *can't* to *won't*. Once he grasps the difference in saying "I won't," his statement takes on new meaning and opens up the possibility of asking "Why?" The changing of this one word often has an amazing ability to make a problem clearer and to place the responsibility for its solution where it belongs.

Impersonal Language

A common means of avoiding emotions or responsibility is to substitute third person for first. Someone who berates a movie for being "boring" is for some reason unwilling to admit that "I was bored at the movie." Students often resort to calling books, teachers, and assignments "stupid" instead of coping with or admitting their true feelings. Some common examples of impersonal language would include:

Impersonal Language	*Personal Language*
People don't trust each other	I don't trust you
My stomach is upset	I'm upset (feel sick)
Some people think that . . .	I think that . . .
Everything's going wrong	I'm frustrated
We're still feeling each other out	I'm still unsure of you
Students are embarrassed to talk in front of a class	I'm embarrassed to talk in front of this class

As in substituting *won't* for *can't,* admitting his feelings places the person within himself instead of having him view problems and feelings as being imposed from mysterious and uncontrollable outside forces.

"What do you feel about . . . ?" "Well, I think . . . "
In our culture the admission of feelings is severely crippling. As a result of this taboo and the exaltation of "intellect," questions about feelings most often go unanswered. As an experiment simply try asking a group "What do you *feel* about . . . ?" and nine out of ten times the question will remain unanswered, although many opinions and thoughts will be expressed.

Have a group meeting in which only feelings are exchanged, and limit the group only to feelings present here and now. The group should help each other stay on the feeling level. Such a discussion is rather difficult, but the rewards are great if it can be sustained.

Cultural conditioning makes such a discussion difficult, especially among males. In *Growth Games* (New York: Harcourt, Brace, Jovanovich, 1971), Howard Lewis and Harold Streitfield report an attempt to have a rather intellectual young man admit his feelings by holding his hand and simply asking him what he felt. The therapist took the man's hand and asked, "What do you feel?"

"Your hand," Adam replied.

"That's a conclusion," the therapist told him. "What do you feel?"

"That you're attempting a demonstration of some sort."

"Another conclusion. What is it you're feeling?"

"Let's see now. Your fingers. Your wedding band. Your knuckles . . ."

"More conclusions. What is it you feel *before* your thoughts take over?"

It took some time. "I feel pressure and warmth."

"It's so simple, the feeling level. But I keep busting it up with thoughts."

The road to admitting feelings is often a long one but one well worth taking and well suited to exploration in group discussion. The most practical guide to such classroom experience, other than personal experience, is a book by George I. Brown, *Human Teaching For Human Learning: An Introduction to Confluent Education* (New York: Viking Press, 1971).

Speech Mannerisms

Speech mannerisms are commonly used expressions which usually make little sense when taken literally. For example, "Let me make one thing perfectly clear" has behind it the implication that the speaker knows very well that what he is about to say will not make the matter perfectly clear. There is no need to ask permission ("Let me . . .") to clarify something, nor is there need to predict that a certain group of words will make anything perfectly clear.

Another example is "Needless to say . . ." If something does not need saying, why say it? Perhaps because one wishes to impress or compliment the audience on its knowledge (which it often doesn't have) or to impress the audience with one's own knowledge.

Have a meeting in which you discuss the speech mannerisms known to exist in the class. Some which might be considered:

You know   (Almost epidemic now)
By the way   (Used to minimize something)
To be honest, To tell the truth, To be perfectly frank   (Implies the
    user is not always so honest)
I don't care   (Often means the opposite)
As you know   (Similar to "Needless to say . . .")
Am I right?, Naturally, Of course   (Often used to impress)
I don't want to hurt you, but . . .   (Oh, really?)
It's not my business, but . . .   (But it is my business)
I can't thank you enough   (Degrading oneself?)
It goes without saying   (Then don't say it)
I just . . .   (Effort to minimize, defend)
Can I ask you a favor?   (How can you say no?)
That's nothing!   (Sort of subtle insult)
As you may recall   (I don't think you do recall)
Do you see what I mean?   (You see)
I wouldn't do it for a million dollars   (Wanna' bet?)
It was nothing, really   (Some people find accepting compliments
    difficult)
You *must* see (hear, read)   (Why?)
I must admit   (Compulsion?)
Believe me   (Implies that people don't always)
So what   (Often simply a mask for anger)
    An excellent, although heavily Freudian, guide to speech mannerisms

is *Mannerisms of Speech and Gestures in Everyday Life* by Sandor S. Feldman, M.D. (New York: International Universities Press, 1959, paperback).

Obscenities

Have a group discussion on the words our culture considers obscene. Start by having each person list as many as he or she can think of. Then have the group try to find what most of the words have in common. Ask why those particular words have become obscene in our culture and what values they reveal. Discuss taboos and obscenity in other cultures.

Because the obscenities are so deeply a part of our culture and so unexamined, they are rich in revealing values. The discussion might be difficult to start. If there is hesitancy or giggling to start, discuss these reactions. An excellent resource book is Edward Sagarin's *The Anatomy of Dirty Words* (New York: Paperback Library, 1962), which traces the history of our common (and some not so common) four-letter expletives.

Also discuss euphemisms connected with excretion that arise in childhood and extend right down to the washroom, bathroom, comfort station, john, jake, lounge, and powder room of the adult world. The closing chapters in Theodor Rosebury's *Life on Man* (New York: Berkley Pub., 1970) should provide fuel for the discussion.

Such a discussion might best be initiated when a teacher or student elicits giggles from some word with a double meaning. Such slips can be turned from moments of embarrassment to learning experiences.

Should

Have the group experience the feeling difference between statements such as "I should read this book," and "I want to read this book." What does *should* really mean? Where do *shoulds* come from? Compare a person who does what he *should* all the time to a person who does what he *wants*. Propose that the existence of many strong *shoulds* within a person is often the cause of unhappiness.

Statements About Myself

This is a tendency which overlaps with "Impersonal Language" (page 47) and is another way to avoid meaningful contact with others as well as avoiding the expression of feelings. The belief here is that much of what people say really constitutes statements about themselves disguised to appear as an observation about something or someone else.

For example if I say "You talk too much," I am not so much making a statement about you as I am about myself. I am saying something like "I feel frustrated that I am not letting myself say what I want to." Rather than expressing this frustration or admitting that I am afraid to interrupt, I settle for the statement that puts the blame on the other person. The important fact here is not whether or not you talk "too much." What is important is that I am changing my statement about myself into a statement about you.

A statement such as "It's too hot in here" really means "I'm hot." I might have heated myself through my own body chemistry without changing the room temperature (food or drink, exertion, clothing, different body position, etc.) and yet the change is attributed to the room instead of to myself.

When such a statement is detected in students, ask them to "put that in terms of a statement about yourself." If a habit is developed of speaking in such a way, communication will become much clearer and students will learn about themselves simply from the change in speech. What sort of classroom comments would this apply to? Most any sentence that does not contain or imply the word *I*.

QUOTES FOR DISCUSSION
The quotes which follow are given to supply leads for further research on the topics touched upon in this chapter. They are also useful in group discussion.

An Eskimo baby who was brought up by American parents would speak English, hate castor oil, and act like any other American child; and an American baby who was brought up by an Eskimo family would grow up to be a seal hunter, to like eating blubber, and to speak Eskimo (Margaret Mead, in *People and Places* [Cleveland: World Publishing, 1959]).

Were he [the American] asked why he doesn't eat fruit salad or ice cream and cake for breakfast, his reply would likely be, that they wouldn't be good, or that nobody does it, or that they aren't suitable breakfast foods. It is doubtful if he could make a Greenland Eskimo or a South Sea Islander understand how cold fruit juice, fresh fruits, boiled eggs, etc. are particularly different from fruit salad, ice cream and cake. The simple fact is that people usually think, feel, and act as they do because they were brought up in a culture in which those ways were accepted, not only as good and right, but as natural (Ina Corrinne Brown, *Understanding Other Cultures* [Englewood Cliffs, N.J.: Prentice-Hall, 1963]).

To the orthodox Muslim our use of pork is revolting, and to the orthodox Hindu, the thought of eating beef is almost as horrifying as the thought of eating human flesh is to us. . . . East Africans find eggs nauseating, and Chinese students have sometimes become ill at seeing people drink milk (Ina Corrinne Brown, *Understanding Other Cultures*).

We consider bathing, the elimination of body wastes, and intimate sex contacts as acts which must be performed in private, but eating is almost always a social act. In many parts of the world bathing and the elimination of body wastes are quite casual affairs that do not call for any special privacy. Eating however is a private act in many societies. (Ina Corrinne Brown, *Understanding Other Cultures*).

The condition of alienation, of being asleep, of being unconscious, of being out of one's mind, is the condition of the normal man. Society highly values normal man. It educates children to lose themselves and to become absurd, thus to be normal. Normal men have killed perhaps 100,000,000 of their fellow normal men in the last fifty years (R. D. Laing, *Politics of Experience* [New York: Ballantine, 1967]).

Everything you've learned in school as "obvious" becomes less and less obvious as you begin to study the universe. For example, there are no solids in the universe. There's not even a suggestion of a solid. There are no absolute continuums. There are no surfaces. There are no straight lines. Why did the chicken cross the road? (Buckminster Fuller, *I Seem to Be a Verb,* with Jerome Agel and Quentin Fiore [New York: Bantam, 1970]).

The development of capitalism brought the new habits of abstraction and calculation into the lives of city people. . . . Capitalism turned people from tangibles to intangibles. . . . The 'economy of acquisition,' which had hitherto been practiced by rare and fabulous creatures like Midas and Croesus, became once more the everyday mode: it tended to replace the direct 'economy of needs' and to substitute money-values for life-values. The whole process of business took on more and more an abstract form; it was concerned with non-commodities, imaginary futures, hypothetical gains (Lewis Mumford, *Technics & Civilisation* [New York: Harcourt Brace Jovanovich, 1930]).

The major task of the American way of life is to keep on repeating to people that they are free, while teaching them to be utterly docile. The chief means for doing this is the system of rewards. The more you accept the assumptions of the system (the more, for example, you accept the principle of competition), the more likely our advancement will be. Moreover, the easiest way to end complaints about the system is to raise people's salary by a thousand dollars or so a year. It is not necessary to use a Gestapo to attain conformity; one may just as easily attain it by paying good rewards. In place of bread and circuses, modern technology pacifies our people with cars and color television (Michael Novak, *A Theology for Radical Politics* [New York: Herder and Herder, 1969]).

If one is free to choose at all, it is within areas defined by a consumer-war economy: schools more or less inferior; draft, reserve, or education until overage; one occupation or another whose benefit is more operational than human; suburban boxes and squares of lawn or apartment ghettos in the central city; this or that vacation, depending on one's status; cars obsolescent before they are driven; and on and on (Philip Berrigan, *A Punishment For Peace* [New York: Macmillan, 1969]).

You consider yourself odd at times, you accuse yourself of taking a road different from most people. You have to unlearn that. Gaze into the fire, into the clouds, and as soon as the inner voices begin to speak, surrender to them, don't ask first whether it's permitted or would

please your teachers or father, or some god. You will ruin yourself if
you do that (Hermann Hesse, *Demian* [New York: Harper & Row,
1965]).

Capitalist development inevitably produces development at one pole
and under-development at the other. The advanced capitalist countries
and the underdeveloped countries are not two separate worlds; they are
the top and bottom sides of one and the same world (Paul Sweezy,
"The Future of Capitalism," in *To Free a Generation*, D. Cooper, ed.
[New York: Collier, 1969]).

Our language, after all, is a thought trap: when certain sorts of notions
don't fit into its framework they remain unrecognized. It's a monstrous
handicap. We are so crippled we haven't even the words to think about
all those thoughts that might-have-been. . . . As it stands, we are har-
nessed to a tongue that's actually doing bad things to us. Much of our
tradition-bound speech is structured in a way that creates a polarity between us and everyone (and everything) else (William Hedgepeth in
 "Growl to Me Softly and I'll Understand," *Look,* 13 January 1970).

No person with a strongly developed aesthetic sense, a love of nature,
a passion for music, a desire for reflection, or a strongly marked independence, could possibly be happy or contented in a factory or
white-collar job. Hence these characteristics must be snuffed out in
school. . . . Taste must be lowered and vulgarized, internal reflection
must be minimized, feeling for beauty cut off. All of these processes
are begun in school and then carried into later life in the case of those
who are destined for the lower half of the nation's productive force
(Charles Reich, *The Greening of America* [New York: Random House,
1971]).

Prostitution was not always the despised and hidden thing that it has
become today. Its origin, indeed, is as lofty as could be. Originally the
prostitute was a priestess dedicated to a god or a goddess, and in serv-
ing the passing stranger she was performing an act of worship. In those
days she was treated with respect, and while men used her they hon-
oured her (Bertrand Russell, *Marriage and Morals* [New York: Bantam,
1959]).

By no means do all peoples take love seriously. There are societies in which love is regarded as a rare form of insanity. There are other societies which have no word for love except as a euphemism for sexual desire. There are still other societies which speak simply of sexual desire, and have no word for love in their language (Snell Putney and Gail Putney, *The Adjusted American* [New York: Harper & Row, 1964]).

This fundamental possibility of choosing suicide, this liberty of man to decide whether he shall be at all, distinguishes his being from all other kinds of being and marks its contrast with the mode of being of animals (Viktor Frankl, *The Doctor and the Soul* [New York: Knopf, 1965 Rev. ed.]).

Food is always a symbol of the mother, since the mother is the primary food giver. Mothers accept this symbolic relationship when they take the refusal of food as a personal rejection. By the same token, some mothers derive a personal satisfaction from the child's eating, as if the child's eating was an expression of love and respect for the mother. Very early in the life of most children food becomes identified with love. To eat becomes an expression of love; not to eat is an expression of rebellion. Very often the child realizes that not eating is one way to get back at an obsessive mother (Alexander Lowen, *Betrayal of the Body* [New York: Macmillan, 1966]).

The concept of mental illness is analogous to that of witchcraft. In the fifteenth century, men believed that some persons were witches, and that some acts were due to witchcraft. In the twentieth century, men believed that some people are insane, and that some acts are due to mental illness (Thomas S. Szasz, *The Manufacture of Madness* [New York: Harper & Row, 1970]).

In polls, respondents often are asked to choose from a list of adjectives the ones which best describe the people of another nation. In 1942, the first three adjectives chosen to characterize the Germans and the Japanese were: warlike, treacherous and cruel. Not one of these adjectives was among the top three describing the Russians, but by 1966, all three adjectives had disappeared from American descriptions of the Germans and Japanese, and the Russians were seen as warlike and treacherous. Predictably, the Communist Chinese by 1966 had become "warlike" and "treacherous" and "cruel . . ." The American image of the German people is even more remarkable—it has flipped four times in less than half a century. Americans admired the Germans before World War I for their industry, their culture and their scientific know-how. Then, during the war, Germans became the hated "Huns." Next, the Germans of the Weimar Republic, a democracy, were regarded favorably. The Nazis changed that. Today Germans once more are staunch allies, even though many of the government officials are former Nazis. By and large, the Germans today are the same people the Americans hated yesterday (Jerome D. Frank, *Sanity and Survival* [New York: Random House, 1967]).

QUESTIONING ASSUMPTIONS THROUGH FILM

Anastenaria
(See page 23.) A religious ritual practiced today in Greece challenges the rational, scientific view of the world.

Dead Birds
The Dani are a people out of the Stone Age who live in the mountains of Western New Guinea. Their entire way of life is based on an elaborate system of intertribal warfare and revenge. The different clans each have their own claimed territory, and each is separated by uncultivated strips of "demilitarized zones." There are frequent and formal battles and raiding parties. Tribe members constantly man watchtowers as an early warning system against surprise attack. When a formal battle is declared the men dress like birds and swarm out to meet the enemy in a wild spear-throwing fracas. The battle serves as entertainment, business, and simply a part of life. When one warrior dies, his ghost must be satisfied with another death; life without war for the Dani is inconceivable.

Dead Birds was made in 1961-1963 and contains no acting or recreating as it explains the unique Dani culture. The film runs a bit long but is otherwise superb and has won a number of film festival awards.

Margaret Mead summed up the film's meaning when she observed that "*Dead Birds* binds together the distant past, from which the ancestors of our civilization were able to escape, and the future toward

which men—the same men, made of the same stuff, but hopefully possessed of very different cultural invention—are moving. But while it binds together past, present, and future, it also provides a savage paradigm of the fate that always waits, just around the corner, for men, because they are men who fight and organize for fighting and organize against fighting, not like other creatures, but as men."
(83 min., color, CF, UC, CU, NU, PSU, SUNYB)

Decoration
This clever animated film questions the value of rewards. A Walter Mitty sort develops the habit of rescuing bodies of people presumed to be sick and/or dying, rushing them off to a hospital somewhere over the horizon. At first he does it instinctively as the humanitarian thing to do. Soon, however, he is doing it frantically for the approval it brings. The approval is symbolized by the medals he keeps bringing back from his missions of mercy. Eventually, he adds so many medals to his chest that they weigh him down and form the metal coffin in which he is interred. Workmen then feed the medal encrusted hero into a machine that turns out more medals for future heroes. The moral of the story? Heroism leads to the scrap heap? Rewards destroy? Virtue is for the junk man?
(7 min., color, animation, MMM)

Evolution of a Yogi
(See page 24.) How a college professor unlearned Western tradition and became a guru.

Flatland
(See page 25.) An archetypical parable of the genius, nonconformist, creator. A two-dimensional creature tries to explain the existence of a third dimension to his elders but winds up in jail.

Holy Ghost People
Take a group of people with a literal interpretation of the Bible, a belief in miracles, and an acceptance of Dionysian worship and you have "holy rollers." *Holy Ghost People* is a stark *cinema-verité* study of a worship meeting of the holiness church in Scrabble Creek, West Virginia. At the worship there is no appointed minister; whomever the

spirit moves to speak does so. The emphasis is on freedom to worship in whatever way one is moved—babbling, singing or playing music, shouting, or convulsions and dancing. The self-appointed minister for the evening sets the tone when he proclaims, "Just be yourself, obey the Lord. Just be yourself. Don't come to church and just sit down and depend on the other fellow to provide the preaching."

There are prayer requests, tongue speaking and even a collection for a needy worshipper. Rattlesnakes are introduced as a test of faith, "If God does not want me to die by snake bite he will not let me die," defiantly announces one man. As the film ends a snake does bite a man's hand, and it begins to swell. Freeze frame, end film.
(53 min., b&w, CF, NYU, UM, UC)

The Invention of Adolescence
(See page 81.) Adolescents didn't always exist—we invented them.

Magic Machines
When we adults put aside the things of a child we made a mistake; we snuffed out part of our humanity. But that was the price we were willing to pay for the mixed blessings of maturity. Julian Huxley said that to call a person "mature" is something of an insult. I think Mr. Huxley would enjoy *Magic Machines;* so do most viewers.

Robert Gilbert is a 25-year-old sculptor who takes what society labels junk and turns it into magic machines which bring fantasy to life. "I like fantasy, it's realer than most of the reality. . . . I'm a child, I never grew up. . . . I'm not planning on growing up."

Gilbert's kinetic sculptures are toys as well as social commentary. The *Knight of Fantasy* questions the division between reality and un-reality, the *Rape of the Flower* confronts the values of technological "progress," and *June 23* portrays police brutality.

Gilbert narrates the film, and his works are allowed to speak for themselves through imaginative cinematography. The film won an Academy Award in 1970.
(14 min., color, LCA, ROA, UM)

Obedience
This film is not important because of how it was made; it is important simply because it was made. *Obedience* shows an experiment in which

average people seem to turn into sadists simply in the name of obedience. The film remains as one of the most useful classroom films for the discussion of conformity and self-direction.

The experiment involves three people: the experimenter, his accomplice who pretends to be a student, and an unsuspecting subject who becomes a teacher. The subject believes the experiment to be a test of learning ability rather than of obedience. The student-accomplice is seated in a separate room with electrodes attached to his arms. The teacher-subject is then told to "teach" the student to answer questions correctly by punishing him when he answers wrong. The means of punishment? The student administers electric shocks for each wrong answer, the shocks ranging in intensity from mild to near fatal. What the subject does not know is that the electrodes are "dead" and the pseudo student feels no pain. The experiment determines just how far people will go in hurting others. Two switches on the shock generator were marked only as "XXX."

In one wrenching sequence the agonizing screams and desperate pleas from the pseudo student cause tension but do not stop the subject from giving increasingly stronger shocks.

One observer of the experiments later commented, "I observed an initially poised businessman enter the laboratory smiling and confident. Within 20 minutes he was reduced to a twitching, stuttering wreck, who was rapidly approaching a point of nervous collapse. He constantly pulled on his earlobe and twisted his hands. At one point he pushed his fist into his forehead and muttered, 'Oh God, let's stop it.' And yet he continued to respond to every word of the experimenter, and obeyed to the end."

Sixty percent of the subjects obeyed completely.

The film comes with a guide and discussion questions. The experiment was conducted at Yale by Stanley Milgram.

(45 min., b&w, NYU, NU, UM)

The Overpass

A series of true events becomes a parable about social order. People in one section of a town have to cross railroad tracks on their way to and from work and shopping. Without street or pedestrian crossing, they simply make sure no train is coming, and dart across the tracks. A letter to the mayor points out that such a condition is dangerous and that an overpass should be built for the pedestrians' safety. The overpass is constructed, but the people continue to cross the tracks the shorter way. Soon the bridge is deserted. In order to encourage use of the bridge, barbed wire is strung along the edge of the tracks. But this is eventually cut and again pedestrians ignore the overpass. Finally sentries are posted to enforce the use of the bridge, but citizens complain that such tactics are an insult to their freedom. So the sentries are removed, the wire torn down, and the people once again dangerously and happily cross the tracks on foot.

The film ends with the person who wrote the original letter now observing that so many people can't be wrong; it must be the overpass that's wrong. And so the structure is torn down. This Zagreb film is an excellent satire on law-'n'-order, freedom vs. the law, and the psychology of people-control.

(14 min., b&w, CF)

People Out of Time
The Australian Bindibu tribe live a Stone Age existence in one of the most arid and harsh areas of the world—the Great Sandy Desert of Australia. The tribe was undiscovered by the white man until the end of the nineteenth century.

The people wear little or no clothing and seem constantly encrusted with dust. Yet they have survived for centuries where few others could live for weeks. They eat lizards raw, work six full days to make a spear thrower, and direct every action at achieving survival with the least possible effort. The narrator (British accent) calls their solution a manipulation of the environment rather than a subduing; their sophistication is one of extreme simplicity.

At the film's end the narrator observes that there is no point in taking the people from the life they live, even if by our standards it is harsh. The people are at peace, "noble savages" with no desire to accompany the white man out of the desert. For the Bindibu, the white man had nothing to offer.

(30 min., color, Time-Life)

The Things I Cannot Change
This National Film Board of Canada documentary is about a family of twelve that has every reason to be miserable, violent, defiant, and just

plain wretched but instead is wonderfully happy. The *cinema-verité* camera observes the Baily family for three weeks and involves the viewer painfully with the family's struggle to survive. Kenneth Baily works only irregularly on the waterfront where "it's dog eat dog." He admits that he cannot afford another child but simply likes kids so keeps having them. The tenth arrives during the time covered by the film. They survive with the help of old bread from a local convent, lots of potatoes, and emphasis on love and affection instead of money and status.

Mr. Baily earned $1,200 the previous year, and prospects for more in the future are almost nonexistent. He wryly observes that their society is one in which "capitalists capitalize on the poor but the poor never capitalize on the rich." He is able to accept his situation with the wisdom of a wall plaque which asks for "the courage to change what I can, the patience to live with the things I cannot change, and the wisdom to tell the difference."

The Bailys challenge the values in a society which claims that happiness needs money and things to grow. The film ends with the family's plight even more hopeless than in the beginning. At the film's end they have an empty refrigerator, a new baby, a few dollars, and much love. (55 min., b&w, CF)

The Ultimate Trip

The Ultimate Trip is a 30-minute portion of NBC's *First Tuesday* TV show devoted to the rebirth of radical Christianity in the form of the "Jesus freaks."

The film follows a group which calls itself the Children of God. Most were heavy drug users but have now replaced speed and heroin with a belief in Jesus Christ as the ultimate trip. In the same way that Richard Alpert traded drugs for mysticism (see *The Evolution of a Yogi*, p. 24), the Jesus people have turned from drugs to Jesus. The group lives communally at their "Texas Soul Clinic"; marriage is permitted only within the group, and morality is strict and traditional. There is no private property, and working for money is considered "unchristian and unrevolutionary." The group logs 70,000 miles a year preaching, always ignoring the established church which it considers hypocritical. They live in unquestioning obedience to a "divinely inspired elder" and spend a minimum of six hours daily in Bible study. In spite of the strict regimen they claim a dropout rate of only 15%.

A Black ex-militant at one of the group's permanent outposts in Cincinnati tells how he changed from hatred to love, "a love where you sit down and help someone and stay with him." Jesus turned him on to love: the same Jesus he describes as a "dirty funky degenerate hippie out of the slums of Galilee."

Many students simply refuse to believe what the film shows, while others consider it another sign of the growing insanity of weird youth. (30 min., color, NBC, Pyramid)

Why Man Creates
This film really needs no description here. Most any public film library has the film available. Saul Bass was commissioned by Kaiser Aluminum to produce a cinematic exploration of man's creativity. His final product embodies the meaning of creativity as well as it explains it. If you haven't yet seen *Why Man Creates,* by all means catch it next time around.
(25 min., color, Pyramid, UM, CU, NU, WU, PSU)

BIBLIOGRAPHY
The following books and authors are all mind stretchers. All are available in paperback and make excellent additions to school or class libraries.

The Adjusted American: Normal Neuroses in the Individual and Society by Snell and Gail Putney (New York: Harper & Row, 1964). The Putneys challenge just about everything that is sacred in American belief—even love. They claim that marriages fail *because* they are based on love, that parental love all but destroys children, that the most serious sort of conformity goes all but unnoticed, and that being normal is equivalent to being neurotic. Readable, quotable, and debatable.
Culture and Commitment by Margaret Mead (Garden City, N.Y.: Doubleday, 1970). I find Margaret Mead frustrating to read but like her ideas. In this book the basic theory is that our culture is entering a phase in which the old learn from the young. An idea worth exploring in a class situation. Other Mead books are valuable for high school students, especially *Coming of Age in Samoa, Growing Up in New Guinea* and *Male and Female.*

Dynamics of Change by Don Fabun (Englewood Cliffs, N.J.: Prentice-Hall, 1967) is now available in paperback. The book was originally six issues of *Kaiser Aluminum News* and distributed free on request. The six topics of concern are change, land use, mobility, automation, leisure, and the future. I've had sharp seniors in high school steal copies of this one. Not easy reading, but a heavy trip in unlearning.

Funk and Wagnalls Standard Dictionary of Folklore, Mythology and Legend is now available in paperback. The two-volume work is reasonably priced and contains some 4,000 terms that tell everything you always wanted to know about gods, heroes, tales, motifs, customs, beliefs, songs, dances, proverbs, games, etc. As a writer and teacher I find this work among my most used.

Buckminster Fuller is now a sort of folk hero among the young. The best place to get into Fuller is through *I Seem to Be a Verb* (New York: Bantam, 1970), even though Fuller probably wrote very little of it. Jerome Agel and Quentin Fiore are coauthors. The only problem with Fuller is that his writing makes McLuhan seem like a basal reader. *I Seem to Be a Verb* is a fun book with lots of epigrammatic writing and is picture-filled. From this Bantam paperback move on to *Operating Manual For Spaceship Earth* (New York: Paperback Library, 1971; 125 pp. for $1.25). If you've gotten this far you might as well go in for a heavy dose of Fuller in *Utopia or Oblivion* (New York: Bantam, 1969).

The Golden Bough (New York: Macmillan, 1922) by Sir James Frazer is the Freudian casebook of anthropology. My freshman college English professor claimed that no decent English scholar could get along without *The Golden Bough,* especially in poetry interpretation. He was right. There are many existing paperback editions (some titled *The New Golden Bough*) of this multi-volume work. An 800-page abridged edition will do fine as long as it is well indexed. Use the index to find customs, rituals, ancient meanings for anything from adultery and heart eating to sleep and initiation rites.

A work that I find equally valuable (also more recent and reliable) is Mircea Eliade's *Patterns in Comparative Religion* (New York: World Publishing Co., 1958). Since everything in primitive society is religion the book is really one of comparative cultures. Long chapters on the meaning and uses and symbolism of moon, water, sacred stones, earth, woman, vegetation, fertility cults, sacred places, sacred time, and the structure of symbols. Also well indexed and useful.

The Greening of America (New York: Random House, 1971) is the peanut-butter statement of the Aquarian age. Charles Reich is excellent at pointing at the evils of normality.

Eric Hoffer has fallen out of the good graces of youth but is nevertheless a man to be reckoned with. His books, *The Ordeal of Change, The Passionate State of Mind, The True Believer,* and *The Temper of Our Time* (New York: Harper & Row, 1951-67) are all small books that deserve meditation rather than mere reading.

Language in America (New York: Pegasus, 1969), edited by Neil Postman, Charles Weingartner, and Terence Moran is a little-known 240-page hardcover by the authors of *Teaching As a Subversive Activity* and *The Soft Revolution.* The book collects articles on the language of politics, bureaucracy, arts, censorship, racism, self-deception, advertising, education, economics, love, psychotherapy, computers, magazines, law, and more. The essays are short and blend the fine mixture of humor and insight. An excellent book for teachers or high school libraries.

Julius Lester is a black social critic. There is a tendency among whites to dismiss black writers as dealing only with the "race crisis." Julius Lester is as much a social critic as anyone else to whom the label could be attached. *Look Out Whitey! Black Power's Gon' Get Your Mama* (New York: Dial Press, 1968) and *Search For the New Land* (New York: Dial Press, 1969) are both superb. Lester seems to grow with his work, becoming more sensitive and willing to talk to whites. They should listen.

Life on Man (New York: Viking Press, 1969) by Theodor Rosebury is all about microbes and germs. But if you read the book starting with the final chapters, it's really about man's attitude toward his body and bodily functions. After reading *Life on Man* one realizes how unusual are our own attitudes towards, say, urine. He points out that urine has been used for cleaning, a beauty agent, for drinking to get high, and for ritual. Rosebury has dug up material here that should challenge anyone's taboos.

McLuhan has really written only one major work, *Understanding Media* (New York: Signet, 1964). Dig this one, and don't worry too much about the others unless you get bit by McLuhanismo. I've read them all, and most are repetition or works that were published only because McLuhan's name was on them.

Understanding Other Cultures (Englewood Cliffs, N.J.: Prentice-Hall, 1963) by Ina Corrinne Brown is still *the* book I would recommend for students as an introduction to anthropology. The book's theme is that values and social customs are relative. Nicely written with plenty of fascinating examples. Available as a Spectrum paperback, 180 pages.

Values and Teaching (Columbus: Charles E. Merrill, 1966) by Louis Raths, Merrill Harmin, and Sidney Simon is a rather unattractive-looking 275-page paperback containing many practical teaching suggestions for what the authors call "value clarification." Defining values as "those elements that show how a person has decided to use his life," the book gives ideas on how teachers can help students realize what their values are and form a more stable value base. The book has become somewhat of an unadvertised bestseller and can be obtained through larger bookstores or by mail from the publisher at 1300 Alum Creek Drive, Columbus, Ohio 43216.

Alan Watts is very big on college campuses but has not caught on among high school students as far as I know. I think many high school students are ready for his explanations of Eastern thought and belief, especially in the short book *The Book: On the Taboo Against Knowing Who You Are* (New York: Collier, 1966).

VIOLENCE AND THE VIOLATED

Violence is merely the sporadic counter-response when one's humanity and one's dignity has been violated. A culture in which human relationships are characterized by a great deal of violation will therefore produce a great deal of violence.

Harvey Wheeler

Linda failed to return home from a dance Friday night.
On Saturday
she admitted she had spent the night
with an Air Force lieutenant.

The Pratts decided on a punishment
that would "wake Linda up."
They ordered her
to shoot the dog
she had owned about two years.

On Sunday,
the Pratts and
Linda
took the dog into the desert
near their home.

66

They
had the girl
dig a shallow grave.
Then
Mrs. Pratt
grasped the dog between her hands and
Mr. Pratt
gave
his daughter
a .22 caliber pistol
and told her
to shoot the dog.

Instead,
the girl
put the pistol
to her right temple
and shot herself.

The police said
there were no charges
that could be filed
against the parents
except possibly

cruelty
to
animals.

(Excerpted from *Search for a New Land,* by Julius Lester
and published by Dial Press, New York. Copyright © 1968
by The New York Times Company. Reprinted by permission.)

Multiple choice test:
The most violent person(s) in this true story were:
(a) Linda, who slept with the Lieutenant.
(b) The Air Force Lieutenant who took advantage of Linda.
(c) Mr. and Mrs. Pratt who ordered the dog shot.
(d) The police who could find no charges to be filed.

(e) The society which permitted this to happen and offered no corrective action.

At least nobody blamed the dog. Linda must have loved the dog, since her parents decided to have her shoot it as a form of punishment. If the dog had been less lovable, the parents would have decided upon some other form of punishment—perhaps a simple beating or whipping. So you see it's the dog's fault Linda is dead. Or maybe Linda is the violent one; after all, she pulled the trigger. Blame the victim, why not?

The example is not ridiculous. We do quite a bit of blaming both the defenseless scapegoat and the wounded victim when we consider violence. Other times we simply consider the violence itself without searching for causes.

The purpose of this unit on violence is to enable teachers and students to confront the violence in their culture and in themselves. It aims to seek root causes of violence; therefore, it is a study of violation.

What newspapers, opinion polls, political speeches, and the man on the street normally call violence is usually a reaction to some sort of violation. The violence receives most of the attention, and the violation is forgotten until it produces more violence.

If an individual is found unconscious and bleeding on the living room rug after a knife attack, he is not castigated for ruining the rug, he is not blamed for bleeding, nor is he punished in order to "learn a lesson." If a society (be it a racial minority group or students or a laboring group or whatever) bleeds in the form of a riot or destructive action, there is a tendency to blame the social body for bleeding or to call the bleeding "unprovoked."

When violence is viewed as a response to violation, real or imagined, the question of its justification becomes meaningless. Just as it is meaningless to ask if a baby's crying is justified or if bleeding from a cut is valid. It simply is and can be stopped effectively only by seeking the cause—the violation behind the violence.

That most people do not consider the violation is shown in a study conducted by the University of Michigan's Institute for Social Research. The Institute used a sample of 1,374 men selected to represent the entire U.S. male population. The group was asked whether certain actions are violent in themselves. Fifty-seven percent decided that shooting a looter is *not* a violent act while 85 percent indicated that looting *is* violent. About 30 percent did not consider beating students to be violent but 58 percent thought that burning a draft card is indeed violent. Violence to these men consisted not of violation of people or their rights but of acts committed against property. When asked about the cause for the growing amount of violence in this country, 68 percent mentioned civil disorder and protest, and 27 percent mentioned crime. Both "causes" are equivalent to blaming bleeding on an opening in the skin—true, but hardly a root cause.

A unit on American violence that is more than superficial would have to include studies of foreign policy, institutions (schools, prisons, military, banks, asylums, hospitals, courts, the police), consumer rights and safety, big business, media, child raising, and the pressures for conformity in life-styles. A study of violence could very likely begin with considerations of riots, war, student "unrest," crime in the streets, etc., but if such a study would go no further it would itself be a subtle "violation" of students' rights to understanding.

VIOLENCE AND HISTORY COURSES
High school history textbooks seem blissfully unaware that America has a violent heritage. America is consistently presented as the "good guys" who would never violate the rights of others. A brief study of nine randomly selected U.S. history texts much used in schools revealed that not one even mentioned the waves of domestic violence which form a very important part of our past. These books devote considerable space to our various wars, always presenting us as defenders of our own or someone else's freedom.

To the impartial and historically informed reader, history textbooks are little more than propaganda pieces written with the good intentions of instilling a sense of patriotism. What they accomplish, in fact, is to prolong and strengthen prejudice and to blind us to the weaknesses of our own system of government.

Students fed such propaganda from first grade on have little free choice by the time they arrive in high school. Here again what is needed is not more repetition of the same old history, but rather unlearning. Unlearning does not mean teaching a history course in which the only content is what America has done wrong, but simply presenting a picture of America that is as unbiased as possible.

Students seem unable to understand why they are faced with the same American history course four times in the course of their schooling. Answers from teachers usually range from "You learn more detail each time," to "So you can learn to avoid the mistakes of the past." Rarely, if ever, do teachers admit that repetition is the handmaid of brainwashing.

In the light of such dishonest history the bombs and bullets of the seventies seem "unprecedented." Most high school students (or adults) would be shocked to learn of the violence of the 1800s or the fact that members of Congress went armed to the Senate and House in the first century after independence, or that the urban riots of the sixties were minor compared to those of the 1830s through the 1850s, or that anti-war protests today are mild compared to the antidraft riot in New York City in July of 1863, when an estimated 1,000 persons died.

In historical perspective today's violence is more a return to normal than a period of unprecedented disorder. The period from 1940 to the 1950s was one of the least domestic violence in our history. Those raised in comparative domestic peace believed this absence of strife to be normal, and this mistaken belief is supported by dishonest history courses.

Our history comforts us while our newspaper headlines frighten. We are inspired by our historic heroes but confused by the murder of three leaders who stood before the world as bearers of American ideals. We are proud of our winning streak in wars but unable to understand the devastation of a tiny country on the other side of the world. We consider ourselves peaceful but are shocked to learn that we have a murder rate forty-eight times higher than comparable countries. We are taught that we are just and yet have continually violated the rights of blacks, chicanos, and Indians. We are the only country ever to drop an atomic bomb on human beings, and we now stockpile twenty tons of explosives for every pound of American flesh. We are frightened, confused, and susceptible to violence.

Our history in school has not provided us with a consistent self-image. The mirror is cracking, and occasionally we encounter young people who have seen through the propaganda, and they reflect back to us what we really are. We don't like our real image; we try to break the mirror. The bearer of truth must be silenced, slain if necessary, and then the mirror will be mended.

VIOLENCE IN THE SCHOOL SYSTEM

We have described violence as the violation of human beings. In any school situation the best place to begin to do something about violence is in the school itself. Violence in school does not mean the two boys in the back of the room who start a fist fight after verbal abuse; they probably need boxing gloves more than a trip to the dean's office. The violence that should be considered carefully in the school is that which is inherent in the system.

Such structured violence often includes: narrowly defined compulsory schooling; the lack of constitutional rights for children and adolescents once inside school; the suppression of religious expression; the censorship of student publications; the confinement of student leadership to a puppet government (student council); the prior censorship of candidates for the puppet government through teacher vote or conduct requirements; the existence of permanent records unavailable to the students themselves; the rigid classification by tracks based on limited skills; the arbitrariness of punishment administered by teachers and administration; the lack of a comfortable environment for learning; the lack of freedom of choice about subject matter; and the almost total absence of significant decisions reached in a democratic manner.

By being violent itself school teaches that violating rights is acceptable if it is for a good cause—like efficiency or education. Schools cannot help but bear some of the guilt for producing people who would agree to fight in Vietnam and once there obediently follow orders that violated the right to life of the innocent. They must share the guilt for a large number of young people who believe it is normal to kill others when told to do so by adults with "authority" and view those who refuse to do such killing as radical, unusual, or cowardly.

A young person grows up in a family environment that is usually far from democratic; he goes to a school in which he learns about the democratic process from books but finds it nonexistent in practice; he is then sent through a military system which believes that democracy is not efficient enough to win wars. After the military he is "discharged" into a society he has been told is democratic and is expected to act and strengthen that democracy. But he has experienced nothing but authoritarian, autocratic rule and so has no real knowledge of nor confidence in democracy.

He looks back and views his own violation (he doesn't use that word, preferring instead *training* or even *schooling*) as perhaps painful but necessary, even good. In his backward glance, he sees others crying out and bleeding when violated. He is angry at them for bleeding.

POSSIBLE CLASSROOM ACTIVITIES

Value Visualization
See page 42 for a description of the "Value Visualization" technique. To apply the technique to a unit on violation, simply change the items to which participants respond.
Sample items:
(a) Robbers hold up a large department store several times during the course of a year and steal a total of $82,000. They injure no one in their robberies.
(b) Employees of a large department store take home enough merchandise so that the store loses $100,000 worth of goods a year.
(a) A husband and wife become angry with each other and have verbal fights about once a month.
(b) A husband and wife become angry with each other about once a month, but manage to preserve calm by taking out their anger in other ways.
(a) A group of policemen get together and secretly execute criminals who have received lenient treatment from the courts.
(b) A branch of an organized crime syndicate eliminates police officers who give them too much trouble.
(a) A group of apartment building managers band together and agree to keep foreigners out of their buildings for fear of damage to their property and decreased rental rates.
(b) A citizens' group composed of foreigners discriminated against in housing breaks windows in apartments where they are kept out.

Starpower
See page 190 for a complete description of the game. If the game is taken seriously, there will often be a segment of those with few points who will resort to some type of force in an attempt to better their situation. Such action is a clear example of "violence" as a response to violation. Those who have all the points will use the power of law and in so doing often become quite violent, in the sense of violence as a violation, with-

out ever lifting a finger. The possibilities of discussion and feeling processing are nearly unlimited in this game. Allow plenty of time for playing and even more time for dealing with the feelings and actions the game produces.

Simulate Violation

Pick a specific and natural minority which exists within a class (a certain clique, the athletes, intellectuals, those in the front or rear, boys with short hair, etc.) and deal with them unfairly. The violations administered to this group should not be serious, but should be recognizable by all. The selection of the group and the existence of the experiment should not be known by anyone. Carry out this selective policy long enough to allow the group to feel that it is being victimized. After the days or weeks necessary, explain the intentional mistreatment, and have the group and the rest of the class analyze what happened.

Anger

Equating the emotion of anger with violence is a common cultural tendency. In a school the expression of strong emotions, especially anger, is either forbidden or restricted to teachers. Yet anger is a basic emotion that needs expression. Unexpressed anger results in blocked or partial emotions ranging from worry and depression to guilt and the inability to sleep. Everett Shostrom in *Man the Manipulator* correctly states: "A person can never have a true and lasting relationship with another until he is able to fight with him. When we're able to show we are angry, that we are afraid, that we can be hurt and can trust—then we can love."

If a teacher has a good rapport with a group, discussion of anger can be most useful. Such a discussion could flow from a time when one or more persons in the class are genuinely angry and allow themselves to show the emotion. A flare-up between two students can be one of the most helpful learning situations imaginable.

The goal of a study of anger would be to help each person in the class accept his own anger, to realize that the exchange of emotion in anger is a valuable form of communication and that a stance such as "I never get angry" is a form of self-deception rather than a virtue.

Highly recommended for background to such a discussion are the books *Man the Manipulator* by Everett L. Shostrom (New York: Bantam Books, 1968) and *The Angry Book* by Theodore Isaac Rubin (New York: Collier Books, 1969). *Man the Manipulator* could serve as a good student text.

IDEAS FOR DISCUSSION, RESEARCH, OR CONTEMPLATION
The Black Man is one of the least violent people on earth. Black Power is the discovery by articulate blacks that they have not been violent enough in a nation that is obsessed with violence.

Americans commit twice as many assaults as Frenchmen, three times as many rapes as Italians, and five times as many murders as Englishmen on a per capita basis. Our gun murder rate is forty-eight times higher than that of comparable countries. We were the first and only country to drop an atom bomb on human beings.

The public fears most those crimes which occur least often. One is more likely to be victimized by a "friend" or relative than a stranger. The closer the relationship, the greater the hazard. In one sense the greatest threat to anyone is himself, since suicides are more than twice as common as homicides.

Violence is profitable. The manufacture of violence machinery absorbs the overwhelming majority of our national budget. The violence industry has developed the most powerful political lobby in the capital.

Experiments have shown that normal persons who see a violent film subsequently exhibit nearly twice as much violence as persons who have not seen such a film. Men murdered on the television screen spring to life after the episode is over; all life is therefore diminished (Senate subcommittee investigation of juvenile delinquency).

We tend to speak of man's violence as part of his 'animal nature' or as 'beastly.' Actually man's brutality is strictly human. The extremes of 'brutal' behavior are confined to man and there is no parallel in nature to our savage treatment of each other. We are the cruelest and most ruthless species that has ever walked the earth (Anthony Storr, *Human Aggression* [New York: Bantam, 1970]).

Shortly after the Texas tower shootings and the multiple murder of nurses in Chicago a young man who said he was inspired by these two events picked up his gun, walked into an Arizona beauty shop and shot the five women and two children who happened to be present. Scientific experiments have demonstrated that the observation of violence, the evocation of the powerful images of brutality can arouse susceptible temperaments to commit new acts of violence (Albert Rosenfeld, "The Psycho-biology of Violence," *Life*, 21 June 1968).

Only New York requires permits to own household pistols; only eight states require permits to buy them. Guns figure in about 60 percent of all U.S. murders; since 1900 they have killed 800,000 Americans—excluding wars (*1968 Statistics*).

One reason surely for the enormous tolerance of violence in contemporary America is the fact that our country has now been more or less continuously at war for a generation. The experience of war over a long period devalues human life and habituates people to killing. And the war in which we are presently engaged is far more brutalizing than was the Second World War or the Korean War. It is more brutalizing because the destruction we have wrought in Vietnam is so wildly out of proportion to any demonstrated involvement of our national security or any rational assessment of our national interest (Arthur Schlesinger, Jr., *Violence: America in the Sixties* [New York: New American Library, 1968]).

Rowan. There's plenty of violence on television, but not nearly enough sex. Of course, in America, we all realize that violence is acceptable but sex isn't. It would be a terribly dirty, ugly picture to show two people banging away in the bushes, but if you want to show someone blowing a guy's brains out, that's another story. *Martin.* I once watched an episode of *Combat* and in one hour 53 men were killed. If mild allusions to sex are more offensive than watching all that slaughter, then something's drastically wrong with our society (Dan Rowan and Dick Martin, from an interview in *Playboy*, October 1969).

Contrary to the impression given by the establishment's mass-media . . . criminal hoodlums account for an insignificant percent of the armed mayhem in this country, and the world. Gangsters today are businessmen who invest in armament stock issues. The petty hustlers, the armed robbers comprise less than one percent of the violence (Timothy Leary, "Violence Is Killing by Machines at a Distance," *The San Francisco Oracle*).

The violence problem is simple. If you want to get rid of violence on this planet just disarm. Just destroy all death-dealing machines. Each individual must disarm himself. Any author or reader of this book who possesses a machine-weapon designed to rend flesh is violent. Each government must disarm. Totally. There is no excuse, no explanation to God or the DNA code which can justify the existence of one distance-killing machine on this earth (Timothy Leary, "Violence Is Killing by Machines at a Distance," *The San Francisco Oracle*).

A society that lives by organized greed or by systematic terrorism and oppression will always tend to be violent because it is in a state of persistent disorder and moral confusion. The first principle of valid political action in such a society then becomes noncooperation with its disorder, its injustices, and more particularly with its deep commitment to untruth (Mahatma Gandhi).

Ninety-five percent of all the expenditures in the entire field of correction (prisons, jails, etc.) in this country goes for custody—iron bars, stone walls, guards. Five percent goes for health services, education, developing employment skills—for hope (Ramsey Clark, "When Punishment Is a Crime," *Playboy,* November 1970).

ADDITIONAL TEACHER-STUDENT BIBLIOGRAPHY
   Alternatives to Violence: A Stimulus to Dialogue edited by Dr. Larry Ng (New York: Time-Life, 1968). Full-length articles from Erich Fromm, A. H. Maslow, Morris West, Edmund Carpenter, Dr. Leakey, Alan Watts, Arnold Toynbee, and others. Similar in intent to the Silver Burdett book mentioned below, but aimed more at college or adult level. 156 pages.
   Blessed Are the Peacemakers, edited by Allen and Linda Kirschner (New York: Popular Library, 1971), contains nearly 300 pages of ex-

cerpts from the writings of people such as Robert Kennedy, Bertrand Russell, Albert Einstein, Albert Camus, Mohandas Gandhi, Pope Paul VI, Daniel Berrigan, Linus Pauling, Arlo Guthrie, Joan Baez, Phil Ochs, and others.

Casualties of War by Daniel Lang (New York: McGraw-Hill, 1969). This is the true story of the rape and murder of a Vietnamese girl by an American scouting patrol. The story is told to Lang by a member of the patrol who refused to participate in the violence. The value of the book lies in its study of the reactions of the soldiers' commanding officers when the incident was reported. The book is much more than a war story and even more than the tale of an atrocity. It deals with the values behind men and institutions that perpetuate violence. Very readable and useful in a high school setting.

The History of Violence in America: A Report to the National Commission on the Causes and Prevention of Violence by Hugh Graham and Ted Gurr (Bantam Extra, 1970). A must for any social studies teacher, this 820-page report has a fantastic amount of detail on the history of American violence. Valuable for student research and selected chapters.

Violence, edited by Jeffrey Schrank (Silver Burdett, 1970). This 64-page student discussion book has some of the most compelling graphics to be found in any student book, as well as carefully edited selections from Arthur Schlesinger, Thomas Merton, Arthur Miller, Arthur Koestler, Dick Gregory, Timothy Leary, and members of the violated minorities. There are twenty brief selections which go beyond the superficial aspects of violence.

Violence, edited by Carolyn Sugg and Robert Sherman (Paulist Press, 1970). Another collection of quotes, essays, and photos on violence, aimed at high school students. 140 pages of well-done editing and photos.

SHORT FILMS ABOUT VIOLATION

All the Wishes of the World

The Zagreb animation studio in Czechoslovakia has mastered the art of combining humor with penetrating insight. *All the Wishes of the World* tells of two friends who manage to save an enchanted fish (don't stop reading yet). As a reward one is to be granted his every wish, the other is to have the same wishes granted but in double doses.

The two exult playfully in their newfound power until a rivalry develops. The original wisher sets out to destroy his rival without destroying himself. He is in a most frustrating position.

What would happen if he would wish for half a bomb?

The violation here explored is that of misplaced values. The two compete instead of sharing their unlimited wealth.

(10 min., animated, color, CF)

The Big Shave

Some will laugh heartily while others will find *The Big Shave* utterly gruesome. This film is guaranteed to be the bloodiest ever shown in your classroom. Probably more blood is shed in this six minute short than in any three Clint Eastwood westerns.

The Big Shave is simply a film of a man shaving. He nicks himself slightly. He nicks himself again. A few viewers begin to react slightly, thinking they see something that wasn't supposed to be seen. He nicks himself again, and a touch of blood shows. The audience isn't too sure what to do. The shaver decides that he must reshave. He continues to cut himself while blood flows thicker—he ignores it but the audience doesn't.

Finally he's covered with blood dripping down onto his chest. Calmly he cuts his throat for the final bloodbath. Meanwhile, the audience is reacting appropriately.

The way to use *The Big Shave* is to show it without warning and then to discuss feelings and reactions during the film. Questions such as "Why did you laugh at the sight of blood?" or "Why did you leave the room when he cut his throat?" should get the discussion rolling. A very common audience reaction (especially among boys) to *The Big Shave* is waves of laughter. An honest discussion of feelings and reaction to this film forms an excellent introduction to the topic of violation.

(6 min., color, CF, UC, Pyramid)

Dehumanization and the Total Institution

This film was made for professional workers in the Minnesota Department of Public Welfare. The cartoon features Ralph Spy (patterned after Maxwell Smart) fumbling his way through an investigation of total institutions (those in which all the aspects of its members lives take place, such as the military, prisons, and mental hospitals) and discovering various ways in which the insidious evil agent of dehumanization infiltrates. The film is backed by solid research and yet presented in the clearest of terms.

The film points out how such institutions can violate the humanity of those it is attempting to help. The message of the film can be extended by considering the school, the family, and society itself in terms of a total institution.

Based on the books *Dehumanization and the Institutional Career* by David J. Vail, *Asylums* by Erving Goffman, and *Institutional Neurosis* by Russell Barton.

(15 min., color, NYU, SUNYB)

Each Day That Comes

This National Film Board of Canada production is amazingly similar to the feature film *Rachel, Rachel,* both in theme and technique. Stella is a dress shop owner who leads a vacuous and lonely life, surviving by taking "each day that comes." The film traces the development of Stella's violation from childhood play to one fateful day when she decides to break away from it all and take a train to the big city.

Stella has been violated through isolation, fear of involvement, and overattachment to her mother. This film contains no physical violence but is saturated with the more subtle violations that are the real problem.

Every scene could stand alone for study and discussion. The quick cutting and jumbled chronological order build suspense and make possible the film's final impact. A short film masterpiece and excellent for group discussion.

(25 min., b&w, CF)

The Greater Community Animal

This simple cartoon is a parable of society vs. the individual. The animal (society) has a restricted diet and cannot stomach nonconformists or the highly creative. Such indigestible elements must be subjected to a normalizing process. It is more important that the animal survive than the indigestible be left in such a state. But can the animal survive without the nonconformist?

A witty introduction to the topic of social violation.

(7 min., animated, color, ACI, Pyramid)

Hangman

Since its production in 1964, *Hangman* has become a classic and one of the most used animated films in the high school program.

The Maurice Ogden poem tells the chilling tale of a hangman whose most powerful weapon is the apathy of the townspeople. If your students have not seen this one yet, you're in luck—they should. (12 min., animated, color, CF, MMM, ROA, UI, UMn, Pyramid, CU, WU, PSU)

High School
Hospital
Law and Order
Titticut Follies
Basic Training

These Frederick Wiseman documentaries are the best thing to happen to *cinema verité* since the hand-held camera. All the films investigate public, tax-supported institutions. They are about institutions we have set up to solve problems. Wiseman's camera consistently reveals that the institutions are more problems than solutions. The films move viewers to consider the most fundamental deficiencies in our social structure. Each institution violates as much as it helps.

Film rental fees are higher than almost any other film described in this book, but any of them would be excellent for a school-wide assembly. Showing all four would be equivalent to taking the entire school on a six-week tour of a school, a hospital emergency room, a large city police department, an insane asylum, and boot camp. (Zipporah Films, 54 Lewis Wharf, Boston, Mass. 02116)

The Inheritance

A history of the American garment industry sounds like an unlikely topic for a unit on violation. But *The Inheritance* takes a potentially dull subject and turns it into one of the most memorable documentaries available. The film shows that today's violence is not new to the American scene. It is a tribute to the militancy of those who organized for their rights. It is also a romanticized, one-sided view of the labor movement. Folk music, stills, and newsreel clips are beautifully combined, with a dramatic flair.

(55 min., b&w, CU, CF, MMM, MSU, NU, NYU, UC, UI, UMn, UM, PSU)

Interviews with My Lai Veterans

Interviews with five veterans of the massacre at My Lai make for twenty minutes of powerful viewing. The five relate very normally, even matter-of-factly their stories of what happened on one search-and-destroy mission in the now infamous village of My Lai.

The five all admit to taking part in the murders, but none defend their action. Texan Garry Crossley sums up the general attitude of the GIs when he says, "We felt that this had been happening many times before, and it had probably been happening many times since." He later adds that the Vietnamese are "funny people—they seem to have no understanding of life. They don't care whether they live or die." The other veterans talk about the one guy with a knife who went wild, about Calley, about the general attitude that the babies killed would "grow up to be V.C. anyway." Perhaps the most frightening statement is made by one who said about the soldiers at My Lai, "They looked like they were having a good time."

The film would make an extremely powerful companion to *Obedience* and *Night and Fog.*
(20 min., color, AB, CF)

The Invention of Adolescence

This National Film Board of Canada production explores the theory that adolescence is an invention of the eighteenth century and the industrial revolution. Adults, since the 1900s, have defined teen-agers as socially irrelevant.

Kids used to pass from childhood right into adulthood, usually with some dramatic initiation rite. They used to have contact with many adults during the day; they were a part of the birth, death, and sex of a family. What brought about teen-agers was the loss of contact with adults (consider the average grade school), the separation of the place of work from home, and the hiding of birth and death and sex by taboo.

Three centuries ago high school "kids" would have been married and supporting a family; today they're considered only mature enough for football and school dances. They are the nation's largest violated minority group.
(28 min., b&w, CF, PE, UM, NYU)

Mr. Grey

Mr. Grey is an ordinary businessman who dreams of escape from his
nine to five, Monday to Friday prison term. The film shows the conformity of the daily routine from the suburbs to the office. Exaggeration is used to make the point and provide comic relief. Rather than a
documentary, *Mr. Grey* is a portrayal of the feeling of being trapped in
a social role.
(20 min., color, MMM)

Night and Fog

Night and Fog documents the violence of the Nazi concentration camps
in the 1940s. The film is an overwhelming experience and has been
ranked in one international survey among the top 25 motion pictures
ever made.

The camera follows the death journey of a camp victim from his
arrival at camp to his undressing for the gas chamber "shower room"
where the only signs of what had occurred inside were the fingernail
marks scratched in the concrete ceiling. Later scenes show the litter of
corpses as bulldozers shove the remnants into pits. A court scene is
shown in which those responsible for the tortures and executions deny
their complicity one by one: "I am not responsible. I was only following orders."

The film ends with a peaceful spring setting—the remains of the
concentration camp in 1955. The commentary leaves a warning with
the viewer: "Those of us who pretend to believe that all this happened
only once, at a certain time and in a certain place, are those who refuse
to see, who do not hear the cry to the end of time."
(31 min., color, CF, MMM, UM, SUNYB, Pyramid, PSU)

Obedience

Obedience is a hidden camera's straightforward report of the famous
experiments conducted by Yale's Dr. Stanley Milgram. In the experiment the subject is designated as "teacher" and is told that he is to
teach a "learner" a word list by giving the learner an electric shock
every time he makes a mistake. The learner, located in an adjoining
room, is actually an assistant in the experiment and does not in reality
receive the shocks. The subject believes that each shock he gives is
progressively stronger and more painful, ranging from "slight" to

375 volts. Before the experiment begins the learner tells the teacher that he has a heart condition and during the shocks complains, moans, and is finally completely nonresponsive.

While a narrator explains the procedure of the experiment and its various controls, a few subjects are shown who begin to give shocks but, fearing the safety of the learner, stop short of 375 volts. The longest and most powerful section of the film is given to the tormented progress of one subject who does give all the shocks possible, pulling one lever after 375 volts labeled only XXX. He says to the experimenter a number of times, "I'm not going through with it. . . . I'm not going to hurt him." But the experimenter, by simply telling him that "the experiment requires you to proceed," wins, and the shocks continue. The man's body language and verbal messages scream no, but he continues to give the shocks while protesting "but he might be dead in there."

The experiment has value far beyond one man's inability to take responsibility for his own actions; a significant percent of the subjects in the experiment gave all the shocks possible. Dr. Milgram varied the experiment nearly a dozen times, but always the same conclusion came to the surface: "A substantial number of people do what they are told no matter what the content of the act."

The film is extremely useful for discussion, but should be preceded with a brief explanation of the situation.
(45 min., b&w, NU, NYU, UM)

The Reason Why
The Reason Why is a one-act play written for the screen by Arthur Miller. Miller says about the film, "What I wanted to put down are the facts, the way we're made, the impulses of the human animal toward war. . . ." The story involves two men, one the owner of a farm, the other a friend visiting from the city. As they sit outside talking, a woodchuck "damn near big as a raccoon" appears 350 yards away. The owner tells how one year he killed 42 chucks in order to protect his vegetable garden. The two compare killing animals to human warfare, and the owner recounts how his "limited war" on the woodchucks developed into a real hatred until finally he realized that with "what it cost to kill them I could have bought enough tomatoes for the year."

Both men show little interest in hunting, but they finally agree to take a shot at the woodchuck. The owner brings out his $65 rifle with telescopic sight and drills the chuck in the head. "Why'd you do that," the visitor asks.

"I don't know; I probably won't anymore," he replies. But viewers know he will shoot more woodchucks. His addiction to killing is not broken by one more shooting.

The many parallels to warfare in the story are obvious and provide excellent discussion material. The film rates only a B minus in production values, but the story comes through unscathed. Very usable in conjunction with the short story classic "The Most Dangerous Game" and Robert Sheckley's short story "The Seventh Victim" in his *Untouched by Human Hands* (Ballantine paperback). Both stories involve man as the hunter and the hunted.

(13 min., color, ROA)

The Revolution
The message of this animated parable of dictators and subjects is that a revolution is merely the substitution of one status quo for another, of one tyranny for a different tyranny. Well done.

(8 min., animated, color, ACI)

The Selling of the Pentagon
The Selling of the Pentagon has by now established itself as the most controversial network documentary ever shown on television. Pentagon defenders attacked the film despite its restraint in not charging that the Pentagon does far more than merely manipulate the news and promulgate a positive public image. The film could have presented Pentagon spokesmen denying the use of crop-killing chemicals in South Vietnam, the burning of villages, the commission of atrocities, the CIA presence in Laos, and domestic military spying.

In spite of its kid-glove approach the documentary scored heavy blows that American viewers found painful. The viewing audience was told that they spend as much as $190 million a year to have the Pentagon convince them that war is a form of safety, that the Communists have a plan to take over the world, and that the U.S. fights for freedom throughout the globe. Since 1945 the Pentagon has sold the public a bill for $1,100 billion in defense which includes over $100 billion for Vietnam.

The documentary showed how the public-image concept has pervaded the military and replaced "the people's right to know" philosophy. The film showed how the public image is maintained by impressive weapon displays, blatantly propagandistic and untrue films for use in schools (the Pentagon film library far exceeds that of almost any commercial distributor) and a tight control on news released to the media.

The film itself is a form of propaganda even though what it documents is frighteningly true. *The Selling of the Pentagon* is an excellent piece of cinematic journalism and ideal for a study of propaganda, militarism, media control, or simply freedom of information.
(50 min., color, Carousel [sale only], CF, Pyramid)

This Question of Violence
An in-depth NET study of modern violence. Psychiatrists discuss the problem of aggression, and the history of American violence is traced from the pioneers to the present. The film points out that periods of dramatic social change have most often been associated with outbreaks of violence.
(59 min., b&w, UInd)

A View of America from the Twenty-third Century
An NET illustrated lecture by John W. Gardner. The lecture and images are forceful enough to hold the interest of a high school class. The film centers on the struggle between man and his institutions. Much newsreel footage is used as Gardner looks into the future and sees violence, repression and rebuilding in store for us. In the twenty-second century America was caught in a "savage crossfire between uncritical lovers and unloving critics."
(21 min., color or b&w, UInd)

Who Invited US?
Who Invited US? is a one-hour NET documentary that caused much controversy when shown on TV in 1970. Many stations refused to carry the program, the educational channel in Washington included.

The documentary traces the history of American foreign policy from 1918 to the present, focusing on military intervention. The viewpoint of the film is that most of the intervention is based on a basic conflict between capitalism and socialism which dates back to 1918, when we sent 10,000 troops to aid the French in Siberia after the Russian Revolution. We failed and one-sixth of the world was closed to American economic interests. Since then we have intervened when it was in our "best interests"—Cuba, Dominican Republic, Iran (CIA), Greece, Guatemala, Mexico, Honduras, Haiti, Philippines, Colombia, and Bolivia, among others. In theory we do not support dictatorships; in practice this policy applies only to Cuba.

Considering that most high school history texts are a cautious mixture of fact and propaganda, this well-researched but slanted documentary proves most valuable.

(60 min., b&w, UInd)

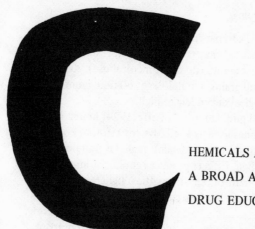

HEMICALS AND THE BODY:

A BROAD APPROACH TO

DRUG EDUCATION

It should be our earnest intention to insure that drugs not be employed to debase mankind, but to serve it.

John F. Kennedy

The Drug Information Test which follows will not test your knowledge as a chemist, pharmacist, or drug freak. It is not presented here to make you feel you know little about the drugs students use. No matter what you think you might or might not know about drugs, right now get paper and pen and in writing answer the questions asked. Do not look at any of the answers until you have completed the entire test.

DRUG INFORMATION TEST

1. Identify the following drugs:
   a. Ordinary form: liquid. Medical use: mild stimulant, treatment of some forms of coma. Potential for psychological dependence: high. Long term effects: insomnia, restlessness. Fatal dosage: 10 grams.
   b. Ordinary form: pills. Effect on brain and other body organs: unknown. Danger: accounts for hundreds of deaths and thousands of illnesses each year. Has produced chromosome break-down and birth defects in lower animals.
   c. Effect: stimulates the central nervous system, inhibits formation

87

of urine, increases adrenal activity, accelerates heart rate and raises blood pressure. Danger: one of the most toxic drugs known. Use: insect sprays (no other medical use). Average dosage: 20-30 milligrams. Fatal dosage: 60 milligrams. Potential for psychological dependence: high.

d. Ordinary form: liquid. Duration of effect: 2-4 hours. Medical use: rare; sometimes used as a sedative for tension. Potential for addiction (physical dependence): high. Overall potential for abuse: very high. Effect: produces euphoria, impairs judgment and motor control. Legal penalties: light.

2. Morphine and heroin are hard narcotics. Marijuana, however, is a _____ narcotic.

3. How does the number of narcotic addicts in the U.S. compare with the number of alcohol addicts (alcoholics)?

4. The U.S. crime rate is rising; this is a time of increased violence compared to the past ten years. What crime or group of crimes accounts for one-half to one-third of all the arrests made by police in the U.S.?

5. True or false: Radio, television, newspapers and magazines are more likely to accept anti-drug advertising than ads for drugs.

6. The U.S. Government makes a profit of several billion dollars yearly from the sale of what drug?

7. Which age bracket of the American population contains the greatest percentage of drug users? (Exclude those hospitalized or under doctor's orders.)

8. More than half of those in our jails and prisons for such crimes as murder, rape, theft, burglary and embezzlement committed these acts in association with the excessive use of which drug?

9. What harmful substance is common to cocoa, Coke and No-Doz?

10. Which drug is the biggest national problem today?

11. Name the most famous American who is known to have used marijuana.

12. A typical American attempt to solve a problem is to pass a law about it. One possible reason for this is that two-thirds of our politicians are _____.

ANSWERS

1. a. *Caffeine* (NB: Psychological dependence—sometimes called

"habituation"—means that when the drug is withdrawn, the person who is accustomed to it will experience psychological discomfort and/or minor physical discomfort.) b. *Aspirin.* c. *Nicotine.* (Cigarette smoking is directly responsible for the premature deaths of 125,000 Americans yearly. The U.S. Public Health Service estimates the overall cigarette-related mortality figure at 300,000 yearly.) d. *Alcohol.* (There are six million alcoholic abusers in the U.S.)

2. non. (The term "soft-narcotic" makes no more sense than would the term "soft pregnancy" since a "narcotic" is, strictly speaking, opium or one of its derivatives.)
3. There are more alcoholics in San Francisco than there are narcotic addicts in the entire U.S.
4. The crime is drunkenness.
5. While these media do provide public service announcements warning their audience about the ill effects of drugs, they make millions of dollars promoting the use of such drugs as nicotine, caffeine, tranquilizers, alcohol, wake-up pills, sleeping pills, etc.
6. Alcohol. (Tobacco is another great source of government revenue.)
7. The adult population. (The average "medicine" cabinet contains a variety of forty drugs. Thus the myth that drugs are used mainly by young people is totally false.)
8. Alcohol.
9. All contain caffeine.
10. Alcohol. (Of all the fatal accidents that occur annually in the U.S., 70%—55,000—are alcohol-influenced. Thus alcohol, besides being physically and psychologically harmful, is also one of the leading causes of violent death. Yet there is little legal restraint on the procurement and use of alcohol.)
11. In Early America, marijuana was used for lumbago, chest colds and other illnesses. According to his diaries, George Washington took part in this usage.
12. Lawyers. (Think of how differently the country might be run if the politicians were mostly psychologists or educators or soldiers.)

If you found that most of your answers were incorrect, it may be because our culture does not think of coffee, cigarettes, liquor, sleeping pills, pep-pills, etc. as "drugs." Drug education consists almost entirely of warning young people not to use (little distinction is made between "use" and "abuse") certain drugs. Other, more harmful drugs are not dealt with in drug education programs since they are considered socially acceptable.

The Drug Information Test is designed to point out the hypocrisy in our common attitude toward drugs. The phrase "drug abuse" as used in schools and teaching materials usually means *use* of illegal drugs but rarely includes *mis*use of legal drugs. The phrases "drug abuse" or "drug education" as used in school emphasize legal rather than medical and psychological considerations. Drug education is limited to discouraging students from using illegal drugs and in reality offers little real education about drugs or about oneself.

A drug is a biologically active substance used in the treatment of illness and disease or for recreation or mood change. Drugs include alcohol, penicillin, LSD, nicotine, marijuana, caffeine, morphine, aspirin, sedatives, and heroin, to name a few. Chances are fair that you are reading this book under the influence of some drug (taken through coke, coffee, or a cigarette) and use drugs regularly.

Over one billion dollars is being spent this year to encourage you to take various legal drugs. Chances are that you are habituated to at least one drug enough so that its complete withdrawal would cause irritation and perhaps even strong physical reaction. Chances are also fair that you knew one of the about 50,000 people this past year who died directly from perfectly legal drugs, not to mention heavy smokers who succumbed to cancer. Or perhaps you know some of the six million alcoholics and problem drinkers or the legions unknowingly addicted to doctor-prescribed sedatives and tranquilizers.

If you realize now that in your own mind you had associated the word *drug* with those substances which are considered illegal in this country, perhaps you could be excused. Perhaps you live in a city where the newspapers give headline space to a teen-ager who plunges off a bridge after taking LSD but devote only a paragraph each to the five who ran their cars off expressways after taking alcohol. Perhaps you could be excused because many years ago you learned to tolerate, even be amused by, the drunk on the street and accept skid row as an inevitable by-product of urban life. Or perhaps you could be excused because drug stores have become pharmacies and executives of large pharmaceutical corporations aren't called pushers.

But it's too late for excuses. The entire country is indeed on a collective drug trip. This massive trip was largely ignored until the late sixties, when teen-agers outside the ghetto discovered drugs other than those used by their parents and started turning on and dropping out illegally. Schools, not recognizing that they were part of the problem, attempted to become contributors to the solution.

The sudden desire for drug education supposedly sprang from a love of youth and genuine concern for their growth; the same concern, no doubt, that gave rise to schools in the first place. Such concern was rarely expressed in regard to alcohol and other legal drugs, for which little education was provided beyond an occasional filmstrip and prohibition on the school grounds.

Automobile abuse (does the phrase sound foreign?) kills far more high school students than do illegal drugs. There are quite a few similarities between automobiles (and cycles) and illegal drugs, and some differences also. The main difference is that one is legal to use under certain controlled conditions after a certain state-determined age and the other is illegal under any conditions and for any age. Schools have responded to the increasing use by students of cars by instituting courses in driver education, required by law in many states.

What the schools have not done is to try to discourage students from using automobiles by showing films graphically depicting the possible dangers of driving (such films exist but are used to caution wise use of the car), or by interviewing ex-drivers who have been injured or arrested, or by calling in law officials to tell stories of their work with "youthful offenders." These techniques have not been used for the simple reason that they do not work. The same techniques applied to drug education do not work either, but are still widely used.

Perhaps schools should not assume that everyone has a passionate desire to own an automobile and should offer courses in alternative transportation (bicycling, youth fares, hiking, etc.). But the fact that cars are easily misused and do indeed kill and injure tens of thousands of teens has not convinced concerned adults to stop teen use of cars. Nor has the havoc wreaked by cigarettes and alcohol caused much of a commotion.

Current forms of drug education (courses, lectures, films) are about as effective as teaching sex education by pointing out the evils of VD. Certainly an awareness of such dangers is part of a sex education course, but hardly its core. Showing livid pictures of VD sores won't stop teen sex; mangled bodies won't cause kids to turn in their keys; and horrid hospital scenes won't stop drug use. All three—autos, sex, and drugs—are deeply a part of the American scene. Schools deal sanely with driver education and, with the addition of a unit on alternative transportation, come off the most blameless. Some schools are beginning to realize that sex education includes honest information about the enjoyment of sex, contraception, and deep human relations, beyond biology or anatomy. But in dealing with drugs, warnings against illegal drugs and information about their danger is considered all that is necessary for a drug education unit.

One basic misconception influencing drug education in schools is the premise that students are turning on out of ignorance. Behind almost all the teaching materials produced for drug education is the assumption that if only students knew the real facts they would abandon drugs. So the film, booklet, or filmstrip attempts to give the real facts (or the most frightening facts) that students are presumably lacking. The problem is that the young are already fully aware of the dangers involved in drug use (as they are of the dangers involved in autos or sex) and often know more about drugs than teachers or even so-called experts. They choose drugs freely (taking into consideration peer pressure) and with full awareness of the potential danger; sometimes even because of that danger. They simply view the act of drug taking as a greater good than other available alternatives.

Knowing this, there are really only two alternatives left to schools. The first is education which will help students cope with drugs and gain the support and strength necessary to make any such experience constructive rather than destructive. The second alternative is to give what drugs provide through nonchemical means. People do not choose drugs; they choose to experience the interaction between themselves and the chemical substance. If this interaction can be provided more consistently and safely or with greater assurance of possible growth without drugs than with drugs, the drug crisis would lessen greatly, if not end.

In order to accomplish the first alternative, schools would have to lose much of their identity as supporters of the established order. They will have to change values so that a genuine concern for the life and growth of youth takes precedent over the keeping of laws and rules and even the desires of parents. Such an approach, in order to be consistent, would require that schools give counsel in areas such as drugs, draft, alternative life-styles, dropping out, sex, etc., as well as bear witness to immorality in actions that are strictly legal.

The second alternative, one that the drug culture itself is now beginning to explore, requires an understanding of the causes behind drug use. Drugs as a problem will never disappear without a radical restructuring of society. Basic causes of drug abuse include alienation, boredom caused by school or meaningless work, enforced poverty in the midst of wealth, and the failure to recognize youth as equal to nonyouth. The failure of religion, schools, and helping institutions to satisfy the needs of the young can be directly related to the self-abuse with drugs problem.

Until such a revolution comes, or until drug taking is required by law, as in *Brave New World* or *THX 1138,* schools can side with their students and join them in the search for meaning or transcendence or whatever they might seek.

Few drug takers when asked why they turn on will expound on the repressive conditions of society. They will simply say that drugs are fun and available, so why not. But there are two other reasons for the current popularity of drugs that even few "heads" recognize. One is technological and the other cultural.

Implicit in the question "Why drugs?" is the question why now at this point in history in this country. Each society has its own favorite social drug, and that cultural choice reveals something about the society. The opium, hashish, and cannabis countries are generally more lethargic, slower-paced societies than our own. They are also places where the climate is warm enough to be conducive to poppy and hemp growth. The climate in these countries has made living at a low standard and leisurely pace possible. So the environment is favorable to opium, and the people adopted it.

In the United States, the taming of a continent did not lend itself to the lethargy of opium, nor did the climate encourage its growth. Instead grains—corn, rye, and wheat—grew well and were fermented into liquor. The colder climate makes liquor's warmth an asset. Today the depressant action of alcohol on Americans actually resembles a stimulant. What is depressed are the social inhibitions and cultural taboos which make social interaction difficult. Alcohol may have rendered the Indians conquerable, but it helps the white man come closer to being himself.

Alcohol is native to America, but pot and narcotics are best imported. It is only in this last half of the twentieth century that the globe has shrunk. One seldom considered effect of this technological globe-shrinking is that the world comes to us; and this includes the drugs of other cultures. Global transportation and travel make the import of narcotics easier and more economical than ever before in history.

In addition to the improved technology there is a cultural change taking place in the Western world; a change most easily seen in the young, but also present throughout society. Apollo is taking a back seat to Dionysus.

Using the classification of Greek drama employed by Friedrich Nietzsche, Ruth Benedict and other anthropologists and social psychologists have described entire cultures as Apollonian and Dionysian.

The Dionysian culture sees the height of existence in the annihilation of the ordinary bounds and limits of existence. Such a culture seeks in its most valued moments escape from the boundaries imposed by the five senses; a breakthrough into another order of experience. Excess is a virtue in the Dionysian culture; drunkenness is not a moral crime or weakness but an illumination through frenzy. With Blake the Dionysian believes that "the path of excess leads to the palace of wisdom."

The Apollonian distrusts such ecstatic experiences. He declares them immoral, irreligious, or illegal. He stays within the bounds of normal experience and views the breaking of these boundaries as insanity or immorality. He keeps to the middle of the road and does not tamper with the disruptive forces of the psyche.

Drug experiences, fasting, encounter groups, mystical experiences, the occult, frenzied dancing, sensory overload in music and light shows are all Dionysian. They are viewed by Apollonian types as threats to a way of life, if not simply aberrations. What we have here is more than a generation gap or a failure to communicate; we have the rediscovery of a world view.

With the rebirth of a Dionysian life-style in a significant minority of the population on a globe where escape is not yet possible, drugs are inevitable and so is their occasional abuse. There are signs now that the drug epidemic has reached its peak in some areas of society. Many of the most avant "hip" students are already viewing drugs as weird. There are twelve-year-olds in Southern California (one of the best indicators of social trends?) who look upon older brothers who are into the drug scene as squares. Some of the early drug apostles have moved on to Zen, psychic phenomena, the occult, organic living, or even Jesus. Many have discovered that the one major problem with drug trips is that they always end.

The most difficult task in drug education now falls into the hands of parents. The effective and honest approach of parents with a child using a drug is not one which will guarantee popularity with the garden club nor the approval of neighbors. Peter Marin and Allan Cohen, in *Understanding Drug Use: An Adult's Guide to Drugs and the Young,* explain that "Adults who worry about their children must finally understand that our institutions do not help them and usually do them harm. There is no one to help but ourselves, and the task that confronts us is an unfamiliar one: not how to adjust them to things, but how to find them viable alternatives, how to liberate the young from everything designed to do them 'good.' It is not a comfortable nor an easy task, for we must protect and warn the young, and fight, at the same time, for their freedom to experiment and blunder, to choose for themselves."

A POSSIBLE APPROACH

Drug education does have a place in schools, assuming that schools are able to reform themselves sufficiently to survive. The medium of school has to change before it can communicate any message about drugs. Assuming that such change takes place, the general goal of a drug education program should be to enable each person to be aware of what he puts inside himself—from nondairy creamer to morphine—and its harmful and beneficial effects. Drug education as such would be only a part of a course in what might be called body education, physical education (in the broadest sense, not gym class), the physical self, human biology, self-understanding, or health. Drugs would not be a response to an alarming situation but an integral part of self-knowledge seen in relation to other substances that affect the body.

Such a course would best begin at an early age and would aim to enable each person to discover the potential of his body. It would involve self-learning about diet, breathing, sleep, meditation, tension, pleasure, the senses, grace, dance and creative movement, chemicals, drugs, body language, emotions, endurance, mysticism, awareness, dreams, clothing, pain, sex, first aid, and perhaps even aging and death.

For the drug section of this "curriculum" a group would learn about both benefits and dangers involved in most of the commonly used drugs. When dealing with the dangers of drug use, no attempt would be made to equate danger and illegality.

A ranking of drugs in order of their danger to humans would look something like this: (1) alcohol, (2) nicotine, (3) prescription drugs, (4) narcotics and illegal drugs, (5) food additives, (6) nonprescription legal drugs, and (7) marijuana. This list will change and is debatable; but schools currently devote most of their drug education efforts toward numbers four and seven and almost totally neglect other drugs.

The other items in this "discovery of the body" curriculum are currently treated inadequately or not at all in schools. A description of their possibilities would fill another book. Here we will concentrate on the seven areas noted in the drug subsection.

Alcohol

Few drinkers consider themselves drug takers; few chronic drunks label themselves as addicts; and few liquor store and tavern owners imagine themselves as pushers. But in spite of alcohol's classification as a non-drug, it is by almost any standard the most used and most abused drug in the United States. Certainly one of the reasons it causes so much harm is precisely because it is not thought of as a drug and is socially acceptable.

As a nation we consume 6 billion cans and bottles of beer yearly, 50 million gallons of distilled liquor, and over 200 million gallons of wine. Americans average nearly three gallons of *pure alcohol* a year and pay from $20,000 to $50,000 during their lifetime for the depressant. All this alcohol results in tax revenues amounting to several million dollars for most states and several billion for the federal government.

About 85 million Americans use the drug; nearly 100 percent of all high school students will have at least tried alcohol before graduation. One in fourteen adult users becomes addicted, and there are 6 million alcoholics or problem drinkers now in the country.

The illegal use of alcohol (including underage use and the estimated 100 million gallons of moonshine still brewed annually) far exceeds that of any other drug. Police must ignore most alcohol abuse but still make more arrests for drunkenness than for any other single crime—two million yearly.

The cost of the abuse of alcohol is astronomical. It would have to include: inefficiency at work and job absenteeism; the cost of maintaining the one in five state mental hospital patients who are committed because of irreversible brain damage caused by alcohol; the added cost of prisons, where half the prisoners committed their crime while under the influence of alcohol; the hospital costs and pain of cirrhosis of the liver, which is directly traceable to alcohol and is now the sixth leading cause of death; the 27,000 fatal accidents yearly in which alcohol is involved; the one million auto injuries; the damage to the body caused by the drug, ranging from peptic ulcers to brain damage; and the broken families and skid rows.

Alcohol can and does often release psychotic reactions and lead to aggressive behavior or even paranoia. The withdrawal pains (dt's) from alcohol are severe and have killed thousands.

The effect of alcohol, as of any drug, depends as much on the person and the culture as it does upon the drug itself. There have been cultures that handled the drug without great injury, while others have enjoyed spirits and collapsed. Alcohol was around a long time before Louis Pasteur figured out what fermentation was. In fact, its seemingly magical properties were attributed to the gods for a longer period of time than they have been to science and chemistry. Whisky originally meant "water of life," and in many cultures the state of intoxication was valued as a religious experience. Even William James, in *Varieties of Religious Experience*, spoke of alcohol's "power to stimulate the mystical faculties" and considered it as standing for the poor "in place of symphony concerts and of literature."

Drug education in regard to alcohol would certainly have to include some of the information and warnings presented here, but it would also help teach what alcohol can teach about oneself, how it works both biologically and physically, its long-term effects, the influence on personality and environment, antidotes for abuse and means of therapy, and even its history and use in other cultures.

Nicotine
Placing nicotine, the drug in cigarettes, second on the list of dangerous drugs might seem an exaggeration. But an objective look at the effects of nicotine seems to warrant this position.

Currently about one in three Americans smokes regularly, and 5 million people smoke two or more packs a day. Over 600 billion cigarettes are consumed yearly in the U.S., roughly 3,000 per man, woman, and child per year. Cigarette smoking has decreased slightly since the connection between cancer and smoking was pointed out in 1963, but the average adult still smoked nearly 200 packs last year. Half the nation's teen-agers are habitual smokers by the time they graduate from high school, and today about 4,000 youngsters tried a smoke for the first time.

Because of such a huge amount of nicotine and coal tar consumption, it is no surprise that 150,000 Americans die prematurely each year from cigarette smoking. In addition, there are an estimated 300,000 coronaries, one million cases of stomach ulcers, and an equal number of serious lung and respiratory diseases (including chronic bronchitis and emphysema) attributable to smoking each year. Smoking caused one million man-days additional sick time this year and is responsible for fires and countless coughs and irritations.

Each year 45,000 die from lung cancer, and a person smoking one pack of cigarettes a day is ten times more likely to die of lung cancer than a nonsmoker; he is twice as likely to succumb to a heart disease. Women smokers have a mortality rate twice that of nonsmokers and have four times as many strokes.

Cigarettes do produce billions of dollars in tax revenue, but they also cost the smokers $8 billion yearly to support their habit. This nicotine habit is fed by a multi-million dollar advertising campaign which has resulted in an image for smoking associated with masculinity, adulthood, *savoir faire*, and even beauty. Ask a stranger to the habit of smoking if he would consider taking a powerful drug known to have harmful effects by inhaling it through the fumes of a burning plant leaf, and there is little doubt he would at least think twice. But given the cultural habit of smoking, its image, and lack of nicotine education, almost everyone tries it without hesitation.

Tobacco use spread around the world through explorers in the New World who valued it for averting hunger and thirst. It was also used as a medicine and an aphrodisiac. Tobacco spread quickly throughout Europe, where it was banned with little effect. In Russia smokers introduced a variation no longer common—they inhaled as deeply and rapidly as possible so that the combined hyperventilation and intoxication produced unconsciousness. Settlers in America brought the product with them and found the natives using it. Perhaps its ultimate acceptance could be seen in the 1576 ban issued by the Catholic Church forbidding priests to smoke—while saying Mass.

When tobacco spread to Asia some smoked the leaf, but others chewed it. Those who chewed tobacco were those already accustomed to chewing another drug—the betel nut. What this cultural pattern demonstrates is that the method of taking a drug has something to do with its acceptance in a culture. One of the reasons smoking marijuana has become so popular in the U.S. in the seventies is that the inhaling of a different leaf—*tabacum nicotiana*—has prepared the way for its relative, *cannabis sativa.* Once inhaling fumes from a burning rolled leaf containing a drug is acceptable, changing the leaf is a minor step compared to the first acceptance of smoking itself.

The method of taking nicotine in our culture might also be part of the cause of the drug's abuse. A 1958 study (McArthur *et al.*) linked childhood oral gratification and smoking. In the experiment it was found that nonsmokers were weaned at an average age of 8 months; heavy smokers who were able to stop were weaned at an average of 6.8 months; heavy smokers who didn't try to stop, at 5 months, and heavy smokers who tried and could not stop (addicted) were weaned at 4.7 months. Tobacco smoking might be related more to the method of administration (sucking) than to the effect of the drug (a stimulant) itself. Most people find cigarettes a tension reducer in spite of its pharmacological properties to the contrary. Another possibility is that the increased air brought into the lungs accomplishes the relaxing effect associated with a cigarette.

Nicotine itself is perhaps the most widely misunderstood of all common drugs. It is a strong stimulant of the central nervous system. It is highly poisonous and is used in insect sprays. Cigarette tobacco contains between 1.5 and 3 percent nicotine, with each cigarette containing 20 to 30 mg. If the nicotine from two or three cigarettes (or one cigar) were extracted and injected directly into the blood stream the drug would quickly be fatal. The only reason that cigarette smoking causes an extremely slow death is that inhalation is a highly ineffective way of taking the drug.

Dr. Joel Fort in *The Pleasure Seekers* describes the effect of nicotine in tobacco: "Hunger contractions of the stomach are eliminated for between 15 and 60 minutes by smoking a cigarette. Both systolic and diastolic blood pressure are raised by cigarette smoking due to the vasoconstricting properties of nicotine, and the drug is considered a major cause of one of the most serious vascular disorders, Buerger's disease. . . . Tolerance develops to the drug when taken regularly, as does psychological dependence and [there is] usually a 'withdrawal' like syndrome when cigarette smoking is discontinued."

Nicotine use should teach us two facts about drugs. First, that a substance desired by a vast majority of a society will exist in spite of religious or legal restrictions; and secondly, that an absence of effective drug education leads to drug abuse.

Prescription Drugs

A *New York Times* reporter observed a drug education program for nine- to eleven-year-olds. When asked the difference between a good drug and a bad one, a youngster replied: "A good drug is something you eat, like a pill, or an injection that a doctor gives you when you are sick to get well. A bad drug is something that will make you feel better if you're mad or something; then it makes you feel all mixed up sooner or later and you can die."

Use of the words "good" and "bad" is almost always evidence, not of careful moral judgment to follow, but of plain sloppy thinking. When applied to drugs and used by a teacher "good" really means "legal," and "bad," "illegal." Drug abuse almost always means any use of an illegal drug, and so drug-use education is neglected universally in our school system. Teaching which drugs are legal and which illegal seems fair enough, but equating legal with good ignores the fact that about 30,000 people yearly die from prescribed, legal drugs. But prescription drugs are not illegal and therefore do not fall into the drug-abuse education programs.

If only good and bad were that simple. In reality there are many drugs (over 200 to be exact) that have been described by the Food and Drug Administration as dangerous and useless, but which doctors continue to prescribe. The prescription of a drug (especially sedatives and tranquilizers) can serve to hide the symptoms of the patient's real problem and thus prevent a solution.

The use of prescription drugs has more than tripled in the past twenty-five years, so that the *soma* of Huxley's *Brave New World* is nearly a reality. According to Dr. Joel Fort in *The Pleasure Seekers,* "The number of users of prescribed sedatives (some of them falsely advertised as tranquilizers), mainly barbiturates and meprobamate (Miltown, Equanil); stimulants, mainly amphetamines; and tranquilizers, mainly phenothiazines (Thorazine, Compazine, Stelazine) and chlordiazepoxide (Librium), probably is somewhere between 20 million and 25 million. . . . One study of patients admitted to the general medical and surgical wards of a large hospital found that almost 20% were users of one or more of these drugs."

Sleeping pills cause over 10,000 deaths in the U.S. each year, and there are hundreds of thousands of sedative addicts unaware of their condition, even though withdrawal of the drug would produce a psychotic reaction, disorientation, or even hallucinations. Drug manufacturers turn out more than a hundred single-dosage pills or capsules for every man, woman, and child in the country, including, in 1970, 8 billion amphetamines. Federal authorities claim that as much as half of this product is fed into blackmarket distribution.

In reality doctors are given relatively little training in the effects of drugs, but use them increasingly as the basic solution to any illness. More than half the nation's physicians were in medical school 15 years ago, and 70 percent of the existing drugs weren't even discovered then. The drugs prescribed are done so because of massive advertising campaigns by the leading drug companies, who spend far more money on drug promotion than on research and development. Every year each doctor is subjected to $3,000-worth of drug promotion, and finds in his professional journal, *The Journal of the American Medical Association,* about 6,000 pages of advertising—an amount exceeded by only one other weekly periodical, *The Oil and Gas Journal.* The type of advertising is little better than the sex-sells, pie-in-the-sky, pretty-picture type found in magazines for the general public.

Because of current drug noneducation, doctors are seen in the same category as police, Santa Claus, and Superman. Care of oneself is parceled out to specialists, thus contributing to alienation from self.

If drug education is part of a course on understanding oneself, it would include a section in dealing with pain. This section would teach that pain is a form of intramural communication and should be listened to. It would teach that disease is always to some extent psychosomatic and that, although doctors might be able to treat organs and psychiatrists minds, cures often lie outside the range of either specialty. The course would teach the effects and uses of the basic tranquilizers, antibiotics, pain-killers, stimulants, and other prescription drugs.

Today attitudes toward doctors are a carryover from the witch-doctor, tribal medicine-man days. With "patients" assuming greater responsibility in their own cure, lives could be saved both from premature graves and from drug-supported nonlife.

Narcotics and Other Illegal Drugs

Narcotics are insidiously dehumanizing and destructive when misused. Scientifically the word refers to opium or its derivatives (morphine, heroin, and codeine) or their synthetic equivalents. Other illegal drugs include some amphetamines, LSD, DMT, psilocybin, peyote, mescaline, and exotica like morning glory seeds, nitrous oxide, or nutmeg.

Rather than treating each here, we shall provide only a list of the people who have the best information available. These sources are listed in their order of value to students.

STASH (The Student Association for the Study of Hallucinogens, Inc.), 638 Pleasant St., Beloit, Wis. 53511. STASH was founded in 1969 by Beloit College undergrads. They publish a bimonthly newsletter, *Capsules,* which features short, well-researched studies and general information for drug users or those working with drug users. They also have a directory of drug information groups ($.95) and bibliographies on cannabis and LSD. The group publishes the semiannual *Journal of Psychedelic Drugs,* in connection with San Francisco's Haight-Ashbury Medical Clinic (Subs.: $7).

Do It Now Foundation, Box 3573, Hollywood, Calif. 90028; 24-hour hot line (213-463-6851). This nonprofit foundation will help train teachers or supply teachers with information in the form of "no bullshit" pamphlets or even "comix" books. They have a newspaper, a record album of antidrug songs, and excellent pamphlets and speak from the side of the youth culture, not the "establishment." Prices are nonexistent or very low. Right now the Do It Now Foundation is probably the best national thing going as an aid to the individual teacher.

The National Clearinghouse For Drug Abuse Information, P.O. Box 1701, Washington, D.C. 20013 is a branch of the U.S. Dept. of HEW.

My request for information brought some nicely printed pamphlets on sedatives, narcotics, LSD, and stimulants. The pamphlets were more technical than the Do It Now pamphlets and more informative and detached. Their language, however, was more textbooklike than that used by the "hip" Do It Now people. The Clearinghouse is supposed to have other materials forthcoming.

Food Additives and Pseudo Foods

"Health nuts" is the label most often attached to those who avoid sugar, use stone-ground flour, eat less than the normal amount of meat, or eat only organic (nonchemically produced or treated) foods. A more accurate classification might be to group those who follow the normal American eating patterns as the "chemical nuts." Eating "natural" foods is only faddish or crazy when everyone else is on a collective chemical trip.

During the course of this year, if you are anything like that nonexistent average American, you have consumed 100 pounds of utterly nonnutritional refined sugar, a pound of emulsifiers such as polysorbates and mono- and diglycerides, a half pound of gum arabic, sodium carboxymethylcellulose, and gelatin, and other additives that stabilize and thicken food, a dozen chemical colorings, large quantities of sodium benzoate, sorbic acid, ethyl formate, propylene oxide; ever-increasing amounts of butylated hydroxyanisole and butylated hydroxytoluene (check labels for BHA and BHT); nearly a pound of acidulants (60 percent of it is artificially produced citric acid); and pounds of flour lacking enough food value to sustain even a rat for three months.

What is normal in eating patterns is deception, chemicals, and tastelessness. The old cliché about grandma's food tasting better is more than a nostalgic longing for childhood. There is an infrequently noticed deterioration of the quality and taste of food in the name of convenience, profits, and mass production. The illusion of a high standard of living is supported by chemicals and advertising rather than the reality of the food itself. If the pure, sensual pleasure of eating were a national value, the quality of food would improve overnight.

Consider the hot dog. All are labelled All Meat Frankfurters, a deceptive practice which means absolutely nothing. Fat is cheaper to put into hot dogs than meat. In 1950 17 percent of the frankfurter was fat; today the fat content is up to 33 percent, and in some cases even 50 percent. In addition, there is 10 percent water and 5 percent cereal filler ("all meat?") and other debris. So "all meat" in reality means that the hot dog contains from 70 to 35 percent meat, and substandard meat at that.

The inexpensive frozen lemon cream pies are 100 percent pie—no lemon and no cream—just 100 percent chemically pure pie sterilized so that microbes won't grow on it and frozen to last forever.

One final example—bread. The bakers know that parents are concerned about the "rapid growth" and "healthy development" of their children. So the bread manufacturers exploit this parental concern while making bread with increasingly less nutritional value, until it is now almost as plastic as the wrapper that encases it. The flour is refined until it is fluffy white and can be stored indefinitely. The reason the flour keeps is that insects and rodents won't nibble on it; mold won't grow. The simple fact is that the flour won't support life.

To compensate for the lack of life-supporting nutrients the bread is "enriched" with ingredients such as synthetic thiamine, sodium, diacetate, monoglyceride, potassium bromate, aluminum phosphate, calcium phosphate, monobasic chloromine T, or aluminum potassium sulfate. All of these ingredients make it possible to buy bread manufactured (baked is too kind a word to use) weeks ago or yesterday and have it taste exactly like wet cardboard.

Dr. R. Williams at the University of Texas reported that two-thirds of 64 rats fed with "enriched commercial white bread" died from malnutrition. He then tried the same experiment, adding the vitamins and minerals which the commercial flour milling removes, and all the rats survived in good health.

Somewhere along the educational path students should learn about what they eat. They can explore how other people eat, what sort of tastes they have learned to avoid or dislike, nutrition, the production of basic foods, organic foods, and even cooking (not only for girls). They could study about how chemicals affect foods, how to read labels, what foods do to the body, and what the body does to foods.

Nonprescription Legal Drugs

There is hardly a product available that is used by more people who know so little about what they are using than over-the-counter medicinal substances.

A school drug-education program should include a sizable section on dealing with curative substances sold in drugstores and supermarkets. Actually twenty cents of every sales dollar goes to support this half billion dollar a year business—a business built on deceptive advertising practices which enable traveling medicine shows to exist today under a thin veneer of science.

Americans consume 46 billion over-the-counter pain-killers every year or 225 five-grain aspirin tablets for every man, woman, and child in the country. Most of these pain-killers are relatively expensive combinations of aspirin and other chemicals. According to an FDA official, "None of these preparations are known to be better than aspirin for the relief of pain and some are definitely inferior."

Every year 300,000 people need hospital treatment because of the misuse of drugstore products. Some of the drugs available without prescription have a surprisingly high quantity of potent content. Bonine, a motion sickness pill, contains 25 milligrams of meclizine (an antihistamine) per tablet, more than many other drugs that are available only under prescription. In other substances the amount of active ingredients present is so minuscule as to be therapeutically useless. Many of the substances variously labeled as pain-killers, tension-relievers, relaxants, or fatigue relievers are usually less-than-helpful doses of antihistamine, aspirin, and belladonna. They can be abused when taken in large doses but remain practically ineffective when taken in normal doses. Much of their effect is attributable to the placebo effect or to the drowsiness produced by the antihistamine, which allows sleep to work its own cure.

Advertising budgets approach $400 million yearly for over-the-counter cures and have contributed to the drug orientation of our culture. If a pill can solve one problem, as so clearly shown on television and in magazines, then perhaps other pills can solve other problems. Some advertising exaggerates claims of effectiveness (there really is no cold remedy or cure) while others help create nonexistent diseases.

Profits on such substances are high. For example, the ingredients in a gallon of common nose drops (phenylephrine) cost the manufacturer about $3.75. By the time a customer purchases a one-ounce bottle, the cost of the gallon has escalated to $120. Very few industries return as much profit on the dollar as the drug manufacturers. And part of the reason for the high prices is simply consumer ignorance and the belief that something that "works" has to lighten the pocketbook or it can't really be good.

Mouthwash is a common nonprescription curative substance that is used, if we are to believe advertising, to provide attraction for the opposite sex and security from the fear of rejection by others because of bad breath. The mouthwashes advertise that gargling with the liquid will kill germs by the millions; yet the average mouth contains at least a thousand million germs. The body needs germs and microbes to live; a healthy body is one in which there is a balance between itself and its microbes. Not only does mouthwash do no biological good (it does provide a nice taste and some security) but it causes some harm by destroying what should be in the mouth. If a severe odor is present, it should receive medical attention, not be drenched in perfume.

Marijuana

This will be the shortest section of this chapter, not because marijuana is rare, but because it is so widely written about and used that little could be added here.

In some high schools pot is easier to come by than a six-pack, and the administration can only turn its back on such a widespread breaking of regulations. In others pot is still an issue of debate or only of curiosity.

Much is still not understood about how marijuana does work or what its long-term effects might be. In such a situation, in a school where a fair percentage of students do smoke grass, new developments in research should be reported for those interested.

At one time marijuana was considered a narcotic with deadly effects. Lately, unbiased research points toward pot as possibly the safest mild drug available. For some unknown reason, longtime users seem to need less, not more, of the drug to get high. Other studies show that experienced users can drive safely while under the influence of grass and even function mentally better than when straight. Because of the difficulty in conducting truly scientific studies, such results are necessarily tentative, as are those which show brain damage or chromosome breakage among long-term pot smokers.

John Kaplan, professor of law at Stanford, suggested to the National Commission on Marijuana and Drug Abuse that marijuana be legalized and licensed, and sold in liquor stores. Those who enter their favorite liquor store for fermented grain spirits and find Acapulco Gold and Vietnam Green on the shelf would be helped, Kaplan claims, to "be confronted every time they enter a liquor store with the fact that they are using a drug. And conversely it will also be healthy when our young people realize that in some sense they are no better than alcohol drinkers."

BIBLIOGRAPHY
This is not merely a bibliography of books on drugs copied from some ads or publishers' listings. It is a list in which ten books were rejected for every one accepted. The books listed here are among the most useful for educators and students interested in learning more about drugs.

Two books come very highly recommended:

Understanding Drug Use: An Adult's Guide to Drugs and the Young by Peter Marin and Allan Y. Cohen (New York: Harper & Row, 1971, $5.95) is a must. The book is as much about youth and education as it is about drugs. Drugs are correctly presented as a symptom of deeper problems. Emphasis is on communication and mutual support of parents and teens. Marin and Cohen know youth and drugs (a rare combination for authors), write well, and aren't afraid to admit that solutions might require radical changes in both the society and family.

The Pleasure Seekers: the Drug Crisis, Youth and Society by Joel Fort, M.D. (New York: Bobbs-Merrill, 1969), is the second book to read if you only have time for two. Don't let the title (no, it's not about orgies and reckless death-defying youth) deceive. This is a wise book by one of the country's sanest drug experts. Caffeine, alcohol, tobacco, LSD, and heroin all receive historical sketches as well as medical and sociological treatment. Plant a few copies in the faculty room, library, counselor's office, etc.

There are two fine books presenting strong arguments for the legalization of marijuana. The first, *Marijuana—The New Prohibition* by John Kaplan (New York: World, 1970). His argument is that a licensing system for pot would be better than the current laws. A 450-page study, *Marijuana Reconsidered* by Lester Grinspoon (Cambridge, Mass.: Harvard, 1971) is also excellent. Grinspoon argues that there is not enough evidence to justify the legal penalties against grass. There is a long section on the history and preparation of marijuana stressing its pharmacological (rather technical) properties.

For a real in-depth study of pot get a copy of the paperback *A Comprehensive Guide to the English Language Literature on Cannabis* by James Gamage and Edmund Zerkin (Beloit, Wis.: Stash Press; $5.95). This is the most detailed and extensive bibliography and index around. A must for a real in-depth study.

Paperbound Books in Print, December 1969 (try a local library for this one), had an article "The Drug Dilemma" that is surprisingly good and included an excellent annotated bibliography. If you want more than the preceding books, try this list out for size.

If speed (amphetamines) is what you need to know about, two publications should give you all the straight info you need. One is a 16-page pamphlet titled *Speed Hurts* by Art Wiener, available from Drug Treatment Program, 409 Clayton St., San Francisco, Calif. 94117. The other is another STASH publication, *Speed Kills: A Review of Amphetamine Abuse,* edited by David Smith (250 pages for $3.25).

For objective info on LSD, try *The Beyond Within: The LSD Story* by Sidney Cohen (New York: Atheneum, 1964). A good anthology of articles on acid is available in an Award Books paperback— *LSD: The Problem-Solving Psychedelic* by P. G. Stafford and B. H. Golightly (New York: Universal Publishing and Distributing Corporation, 1967).

Drugs on the College Campus by Helen Nowlis (New York: Anchor Books, 1969) is another misnamed book. It is really of interest far beyond the campus and is an excellent general introduction to drug use. Also included is a pharmacological review of several drugs, sections on the response of educational institutions to drugs, legal aspects.

By Prescription Only by Morton Mintz, rev. ed. (Boston: Beacon Press, 1967), is one of the first to document the real problem of drug abuse in the use of prescription drugs. Most of the material comes from the Kefauver hearings.

The Poisons in Your Food by William Longgood, rev. ed. (New York: Pyramid Books, 1969) is a one-sided scare approach to food additives and the food-processing industry. Longgood's basic theme is that poisons are still poisons even if taken a little at a time.

The Chemical Feast by James S. Turner (New York: Grossman,

1971), published as a report of the Nader's Raiders, details current chemicals in the food and abuses perpetrated on the public by food manufacturers.

FILMOGRAPHY

Viewing as many drug-education films as I've seen is enough to drive anyone to drink. I learned little from viewing most of the films but a lot from a few.

Most of the drug-education films claim to be unbiased presentations of facts which will enable students to make their own choices. In reality, the films are attempts by adults to keep their children away from drugs. Such an attempt might be laudable if the adults could offer good reasons, true information, and alternatives to a consumer-drug society. But they can't, and so the films suffer.

The comments which follow each of these films are based on information gained from personal viewing, from statements made by a panel of students and faculty members at the University of California and by a panel of diverse people (William Buckley, Judith Crist, Peter Fonda included) at the National Coordinating Council on Drug Abuse Education and Information. (The complete evaluation report of the latter group is available for $2 from 211 Connecticut Ave., N.W., Washington, D.C. 20036.)

Almost totally missing from the list are good films about tobacco, alcohol, and nicotine abuse, as well as films about prescription and over-the-counter drugs. The films are limited almost entirely to illegal drugs and include most of the well-known films released between 1965 and 1971. Omitted are those which are obviously not credible and those which are hopelessly outdated or run-of-the-mill.

The American Alcoholic (1967)
An NBC portrait of the six million alcoholics in America. About 70 percent live in respectable neighborhoods, pay taxes, raise families, and have life-styles which would never betray their problem. An excellent study of middle-class alcoholism.
(55 min., color, MGH, ROA)

The Addicted (1958)
A very good film for 1958. It was originally part of the CBS series

The Twentieth Century and is narrated by Walter Cronkite. The stress is on narcotic addiction, which the film urges be considered a sickness rather than a crime. Content is good, but the same sort of treatment has been done just as well or better more recently. Students today find the age of the film a serious drawback.
(52 min., color, NAVC)

Anything for Kicks (1969)

This film is currently one of the best free-loan films on drugs. Available from National Audiovisual Center, Washington, D.C. (Address "Distribution Branch" for loan or "Sales Branch" for purchase, at $37.25.)

Stills are used to tell the true story of a teen couple who plunge into the drug scene and nearly lose their lives. The final scenes show adult-teen communication efforts. For groups of adults or adults and teens where no budget is available, this film should do nicely.
(11 min., color, NAVC)

Beyond LSD (1968)

Most usable for adults, a mixed group of adults and teens, or a group of parents who fear their kids are using drugs but are unable to communicate with them. The acting and situations in the film are rather phony, but the message is valid. In the face of fearful hysterical parents, a community counselor explains that drugs are symptoms of deeper problems that require communication and understanding to solve. The film paints LSD as more evil than it is and occasionally becomes preachy and condescending.
(25 min., color, KSU, UC, USC, FSU)

The Chemistry of Behavior (1963)

This film was an NET presentation back in the days when NET thought of a television program as a man sitting behind a desk talking. The emphasis in this film is scientific—how man and animals react biochemically to drugs. Best use for the film is in a science class where interest is high; the film does not provide its own motivation.
(29 min., b&w, UC, UInd)

The Circle (1967)

This National Film Board of Canada production is a *cinema-verité* study of an individual at Daytop Village. It follows the addict through the tough encounter sessions that Daytop uses to help an individual accept himself once again.

The film is best used for a group very interested in the encounter group treatment method. Those not particularly interested will often find the film boring and too long. Good room acoustics are needed for viewing. The action ranges from stagy to dramatic.
(57 min., b&w, CF, KSU, UC, UM)

The Current Scene (1968)
Produced by KCET-TV, this film is a kinescope and thus suffers from poor print quality. Concern is limited to presenting pros and cons of pot. Scenes of a pot party, a pusher breaking a "brick" of marijuana into joints, worried parents, and hip students all present a variety of viewpoints. By now it would be hard to find an audience which hasn't already heard these opinions, but it might exist somewhere.
(26 min., b&w, UC, UInd)

David (1965)
Don Pennebaker did much to popularize the *cinema-verité* style here in the U.S., and this is his film of David, an addict under treatment at the original Synanon House in Santa Monica. Like *The Circle,* the film is good for providing an insight into the encounter-method approach to addiction cure.

David is visited by his wife and son, and the Synanon leaders fear this might lure him away from the center. In the end he decides to stay until cured. If the film is used, it should be pointed out that Synanon does not operate this way today. Families are encouraged to live in with the addict.

Technically the film is rough and at times confusing, but it does capture an addict's struggle with himself.
(54 min., b&w, Time-Life, UC)

A Day in the Death of Donnie B. (1969)
This well-made free-loan film sells for only $27. Donnie B. is a black ghetto kid hooked on heroin. The people around him seem either unconcerned or oblivious to his condition. He staggers around, more like a drunk than an addict, looking for money to get his fix, until he

finally wins a dice game and makes his buy. The all-black cast does a credible job, and the film is a rather good scare film. It presents a bleak picture for heroin addicts, but is an effective discussion starter, especially for urban teens and preteens.
(14 min., b&w, NAVC, UC)

The Distant Drummer (1968)
This 45-minute film is actually a condensation of two films, *Movable Scene* and *Flowers of Darkness.* Its condensation makes the film even more superficial than its original parts. The film is not overly preachy, however, and does serve as a general overview of the drug scene. Paul Newman narrates. Free loan from NAVC only.
(45 min., color, NAVC, SUNYB, UC)

The Drag (1965)
A clever and humorous film about the nonsense of smoking. The film tells the story of a chain smoker from the vantage point of a psychiatrist's couch. The film is humorous and could be a good starting place for confrontation. A National Film Board of Canada production.
(9 min., color, KSU, MGH, ROA)

Driving and Drugs (1968)
A free-loan film designed to acquaint viewers with the hazards of driving under the influence of barbiturates, amphetamines, pot, mescaline, and LSD. Alcohol is not considered a drug in the film, and much of the information presented is misleading and inaccurate.
(14 min., color, Jam Handy, 2821 E. Grand Blvd., Detroit, Mich. 48211)

Drug Abuse: Bennies and Goofballs (1967)
An "official government" film, again narrated by Paul Newman. Scare tactics are the main technique, but the film has a few pluses going for it. It does deal with amphetamines and barbiturates which are available legally; it does warn about mixing drugs; and it features an interview between a convicted murderer and his defense counsel, who is a paradigm of insensitivity.
(20 min., b&w, MMM, UMn)

Drug Abuse: The Chemical Tomb (1969)
A collection of all the scare tactics used in films to frighten kids away from drugs. In addition to the scare tactics, the film gives misinformation about drugs. One to avoid.
(19 min., color, FDI, ROA)

Drug Abuse: One Town's Answer (1969)
This film would be good for a group of parents who are pushing for tougher laws to stop their kids from taking drugs. It is about Fort Bragg, California, where the teens used drugs and passed them on to each other. After the parents realized that so many of their kids were involved that laws would have little effect, they called in two re-formed drug users who set up "Awareness House." Much of the film is given to letting the teens talk; what they have to say is not especially valuable, but the fact that they do talk is important.
(16 min., color, UC, USF)

Drugs and the Central Nervous System (1966)
The film shows how aspirin works on the body and then moves on to demonstrate the effects of glue, barbiturates, morphine, codeine, heroin, amphetamines, marijuana, and LSD. The film is visual enough to hold attention but does have a number of inaccuracies. It claims that LSD can cause permanent brain damage, that pot leads to other drugs, that heroin is the strongest drug, and that a doctor's prescription might change the effect of a drug. Combination of animation and live film.
(16 min., color, CHURCHILL, CU, MMM, NU, UC, UM, UU)

Drugs: The Children Are Choosing (1969)
This seven-film series was produced by the excellent TV station KQED and is among the most comprehensive and accurate drug-education films available anywhere. The films inform the viewer about our drug culture, history of mood-changing substances, pharmacology of drugs, how the very young learn about drugs from parents, and the various attempts to help young people cope with drugs. The films are not exactly action packed (much talking), but the information they provide is balanced and accurate. For a brochure on the series write

Extension Media Center, University of California, Berkeley, Calif.
94720.
(7 color films, 30 min. each, UC)

11:59: Last Minute To Choose (1971)
A film documentary originally presented on New York television
that is more alarming than educational. Attempts to show the pain involved with drug taking in an effort to discourage others from joining
in. A well-made film.
(27 min., color, Pyramid)

Evolution of a Yogi (1970)
Richard Alpert, an early assistant to Timothy Leary, describes his own
journey from drug trips to mysticism. For more information, see page
24.

Drugs: Facts Everyone Needs to Know (1970)
If viewers can tolerate a 29-minute straight lecture they should find
this film very informative. Dr. Sanford J. Feinglass has a good lecture
manner and knows what he is talking about. He discusses depressants,
alcohol, barbiturates, narcotics, tranquilizers, coffee, cola, amphetamines, cocaine, psychedelics, tobacco, and marijuana. One of the most
informative films available.
(29 min., color, NYU)

Drugs in the Tenderloin (1968)
A candid look at San Francisco drug users in the Tenderloin District.
The film accepts "freaks" as people and allows them to say things that
many viewers will have never heard before. A poverty worker tells how
"straight" society exploits and ostracizes the drug users, and addicts
point out that drug traffic is a big business that even involves the
police.
(52 min., b&w, UC, UInd)

Escape to Nowhere (1968)
Debbie is an actual 16-year-old girl who is into drugs. The camera follows her around as she wanders and talks about herself and responds to
questions asked by an off-camera interviewer. The film is well done

and will hold the interest of almost any audience. Debbie does come across as sincere, although she doesn't appear as confused and lonely as she claims. She admits to being into heroin: "I'm in too far now, I think I am." The Drug Information Clearinghouse Committee observed that "Debbie's story might mistakenly imply that drug taking is a cause, rather than a result of Debbie's lack of maturity and responsibility." Intercut are scenes such as a middle-aged TV viewer drinking and smoking and shaking his head over youthful drug abuse.
(25 min., color, UC)

Fight or Flight (1967)
This film shows former drug addicts from Daytop Village talking about their experiences. They imply that pot leads to heroin and that pot and LSD are habit-forming and physically addictive. The film was made for the International Association of Police Chiefs and seems to be saying to stay away from illegal drugs. Period.
(15 min., color, J&F Productions, Inc., Suite 700, 1401 Walnut St., Philadelphia, Pa. 19102)

From Pot to Psychedelics (1968)
An already dated film that concludes that drug use is spreading. Kinescope makes for poor quality film, although the opinions expressed by people such as Dr. Joel Fort and Timothy Leary are interesting.
(32 min., b&w, UC, UInd)

From Runaway to Hippie (1967)
This NBC-TV show was originally shown on the Huntley-Brinkley Report. Communists, hippies, pushers, drugs, death, glue, hepatitis, VD, communes, and dropouts are all the same according to this film. The film is so bad and biased that it can be used to demonstrate how attitudes have changed since 1967. Another way to use this film is to show it as "this is the way it really is." After showing it, stand back and watch the sparks fly.
(18 min., color, CCM, FDI)

Grooving (1970)
A group of kids, fourteen to eighteen years old, sit around and rap

about drugs. Some are experienced users; others have never tried it. The general message is antidrug. Adults who see the film are impressed with the kids' honesty (probably "shocked" would be a more accurate description). The teens try to deal with the reasons behind drug use, and the users and nonusers confront each other honestly. At the film's end some of the users appear converted for no apparent reason supplied in the film. An interesting discussion for teens.
(31 min., color, UC, UM)

The Hippie Temptation (1967)
A 1967 CBS-TV production in which Harry Reasoner tries to explain to the vast wasteland what hippies are all about. The film is biased, but should be a good source of nostalgia in 1980.
(51 min., color, MGH)

Here's Help (1970)
A free-loan (purchase $96.25) film that has as its message the fact that help for heroin addicts is available. The film surveys the various approaches (methadone, encounter group, religion, and combination approaches) used to treat addiction. Useful for groups in which potential addicts are present. The only shortcoming in the film is that it does not indicate how difficult it is to become cured or how difficult it is in many places to get into a program.
(28 min., color, NAVC)

Hide and Seek (1966)
A sketchy story of how a middle-class white teen-ager becomes a heroin addict. The idea of the film is to elicit sympathy for Carl, to make the viewer say to himself, "I'll never try heroin." Perhaps the only education comes in a detailed scene in which Carl injects heroin. A weak film.
(14 min., color, Pyramid, UC)

Hooked (1967)
Young former drug addicts who have been off drugs for three months to two years talk about their path to addiction. Some of their stories are genuinely moving; their basic message: "I didn't think it would happen to me." The filmmakers reveal their own prejudice by leaving in

those comments which have a cumulative effect of stating that marijuana leads to heroin. Of very limited value.
(20 min., b&w, CHURCHILL, MMM, SUNYB, UC, UM, UMn, USC)

The Law: How Effective Is It? (1968)
A panel discussion that turns into a heated debate. The panel has Joel
Fort, Joseph Oteri, William Quinn, and others. Opinions expressed
range far and wide and make for stimulating viewing if you can tolerate
panel discussions.
(36 min., b&w, UC, UInd)

The Losers (1965)
An old CBS-TV documentary that now seems dated and superficial.
(31 min., b&w, MMM, ROA, SUNYB, UC)

LSD (1967)
A film for Navy trainees to discourage them from LSD. The main
emphasis: taking LSD might lead to a situation in which one is unable
to fulfill his duties—like shooting people or flying a bombing mission.
Best left in the Navy; contains serious inaccuracies.
(28 min., color, NAVC)

LSD-25 (1967)
In this film LSD is personified by a rather attractive voice. The film
does stress what is unknown rather than deluge the viewer with half-
truths that are supposedly known. It also points out that an LSD reaction depends as much on the person as on the drug. The film is com-
paratively unbiased, but does make many of the dangers connected
with LSD seem like the rule rather than the exception.
(27 min., color, KSU, MMM, UC, WU)

LSD: Lettvin vs. Leary (1967)
Half of this film is clipped from underground sources and shows
Timothy Leary sitting behind a flickering candle flame and urging
LSD on viewers. The other half shows MIT Professor Jerome Lettvin
arguing that LSD is not worth the risk. The film is long and talky
but for an audience with a real interest in drugs it should prove provocative. The rational vs. the mystical—a heavy trip.
(54 min., b&w, UC, UInd)

LSD: Insight or Insanity (Revised edition, 1968)
The film concludes that LSD is more likely to lead to insanity than to insight. It takes what are conceivable occurences or rare effects and tends to imply that they are common. If LSD is as dangerous as the film points out, that danger surely could be made clear without resorting to the scare techniques this film uses.
(28 min., color, CU, KSU, MMM, ROA, UC, UM, UMn, USC, UU)

LSD: The Spring Grove Experiment (1966)
A CBS-TV documentary recording how LSD can be used in psychotherapeutic treatment. The film follows a 48-year-old housewife who suffered an emotional breakdown and a 33-year-old man who suffered from acute alcoholism. LSD is used in connection with psychiatry to provide an emotional release which aids the patients. The film is objective, and rare in pointing out how LSD can be used positively. Teens might find the film a little too long, and some remarks are difficult to hear.
(54 min., b&w, KSU, UM, UMn, USC, UU)

LSD: Trip to Where (1968)
A gathering of evidence which shows that LSD is not worth the risk. Some of the "evidence" is in reality opinion, and the film's most powerful moment is the dramatic revelation of a young man's face, burned when he set himself afire while on an LSD trip. The film's producer admits to trying LSD himself and having a good trip.
(25 min., color, CU, MGH, NU)

Marathon: The Story of Young Drug Users (1967)
A nicely done study of a Daytop Village encounter group. Focus is on five Daytop residents, none teen-agers. The University of California group rated this one "very good to excellent."
(51 min., b&w, FI, UC, FSU)

Marijuana (1968)
This film claims to present objective evidence about marijuana, so that a young person can decide for himself. In reality the film is an attempt to dissuade users from smoking pot. Inmates of a California narcotic

rehabilitation center imply that pot leads to worse drugs, and the film ends with a string of straight-looking youngsters urging viewers to play it straight. Maybe for elementary grades, but no longer credible for high school students. Narrated by Sonny Bono.
(34 min., color, BFA, KSU, MMM, UM)

Marijuana (CBS Reports, 1968)
One of the most balanced films available on marijuana, it was originally shown on CBS-TV. Mike Wallace narrates as varying viewpoints on marijuana use are presented. The emphasis is on the legal handling of the drug, but a brief history of marijuana laws is also presented. One of the best TV films.
(52 min., b&w, CAROUSEL (sale), MMM, UC, UM)

Marijuana: The Great Escape (1970)
A dramatic film about George, a teen-age drag-racing enthusiast. George turns his girl on with grass, and she is injured in an auto accident and unable to attend the big race. At the drag race George himself cracks up, supposedly from pot. The film implies that pot leads to disaster, that it is mainly an escape, that users of marijuana lose control of themselves, and that for marijuana users "work is a drag." The production qualities of the film are slick, and it might be a good discussion starter, even though it isn't highly credible. A reaction like "That was really corny" can be an excellent springboard for discussion.
(20 min., color, BFA, ROA)

Marijuana—World of the Weed (1968)
A rather academic presentation of the history of marijuana. Content is interesting and well researched for a class already motivated. High school and college level.
(21 min., b&w, UInd)

Narcotics: The Decision (1961)
A dated film that would surely turn off most any kid. The film describes an 18-year-old girl's downfall from innocence to accomplice in the murder of a pharmacist.
(30 min., color, AIM, UMn, WU)

Narcotics: The Inside Story (1967)
A film designed to tell teens that narcotics are bad. It presents numerous scientific inaccuracies and would almost certainly be greeted with disdain and/or laughter by a teen-age audience today.
(12 min., color, BV, USC)

Narcotics: Pit of Despair (1967)
After watching so many drug-education films, one thing I've learned well is how to prepare and inject heroin. Film makers seem obsessed with this scene, and in *Narcotics: Pit of Despair* it is nearly the only credible scene. The film contains many inaccuracies (even mentions a "pot needle"), half-truths, and stereotypes. An updated version of *Narcotics: The Inside Story* that is only a little improved.
(18 min., color, CCM, ROA, UMn)

A Nice Kid like You (1969)
A good film which consists entirely of verbal, intelligent, upper-middle-class Eastern college students talking about drugs, sex, college life, and parents. Most usable for adult groups and high school seniors heading for such a college life. The film is not at all preachy or moralistic, and the opinions expressed are often enlightening and provocative.
(38 min., b&w, UC)

Professor Lettvin Tuned In (1967)
A 90-minute one-man show. As a follow-up to his filmed debate with Timothy Leary, Dr. Jerome Lettvin talks before a TV studio audience of high school students. He admits that we live in a corrupt world, but that if young people are to change it, drugs will simply serve to limit their potential and in the long run aid the status quo. The film is long, but still excellent for almost any audience with the time to watch it and the freedom to discuss and ponder.
(90 min., b&w, UC, UInd)

Scag (1970)
One of the most recent and best films on heroin now available. It presents the story of a white middle-class boy and a black ghetto girl. The girl recognizes that "drugs are not the problem; they're the symp-

toms of something in the person." The film traces a poppy crop from Turkey to the New York streets, and shows both methadone and therapeutic treatment methods. The film is well made, accurate, and informative.
(21 min., color, EBF)

Speedscene: The Problem of Amphetamine Abuse (1969)
A physician suggests that even doctors could get along without prescribing amphetamines at all. The message is that speed kills. Period. The film is visually interesting and one of the few devoted specifically to amphetamines.
(17 min., color, BFA, ROA, UC, UM)

Trip to Nowhere (1970)
An NBC-TV "White Paper" on youth and drugs that is far better than average. The most moving and significant scene is an encounter between parents and a teen-age boy who had been on drugs for five years without his parents knowing it. In a psychiatric interview, it becomes evident that the father's inability to express affection for his son was an important factor leading to drug abuse. The film clearly recognizes that drug abuse is a symptom and that adults must share the burden for its cause. Another scene demonstrates how readily available drugs are; an NBC news crew filmed at random in Brooklyn and within 15 minutes had captured a drug sale on film. The drug-education programs which the film presents are really examples of too little too late. A good film for discussion.
(52 min., color, NBC, Pyramid, UM, FSU)

Smokescreen (1970)
An antismoking, scare-tactic film. This film will undoubtedly do little to change smokers into nonsmokers, but it is fun to watch and could prompt an interesting confrontation between smokers and nonsmokers. There is a collage history of the U.S. as seen through cigarette ads, glimpses of surgery, a tour of two great throats, the etiquette of smoking according to Amy Vanderbilt, a heart popping out of a cutopen chest, cigarette ads, all set to "Smoke Gets in Your Eyes."
(5 min., color, Pyramid)

The Ultimate Trip (1970)
A segment from an NBC-TV "First Tuesday" show about the Jesus
Freaks. Most were heavily into the drug scene but have converted
from drugs to Jesus as the "ultimate trip." For details see page 61.

US (1971)
Us paints a background of the soul-destroying cityscape in which many
of us live to the tune of media filled with violence, war, and inhumanity.
Us shows a group of women who deplore the youth drug culture while
using diet pills and tranquilizers, two businessmen who get drunk on
camera while criticizing the use of drugs by both their wives and the
young, a group of engineering students chain-smoking and getting
smashed on beer, and a group of young people smoking pot and deplor-
ing everyone else. Finally, a speed freak, beautiful but destroyed, sits
passively. The film is excellent as a discussion starter.
(28 min., color, CHURCHILL, FSU)

A Walk in the Park (1970)
One of the most unique drug-education films available and also one of
the most useful with a skilled and knowledgeable group leader. The
film is best for teens who are part of a drug culture or for schools
where the students are heavily into drug use. This film, unlike 95 percent of the others, does not start from the premise that students are
ignorant about drugs but adults know the facts. Adults will find this
film difficult to handle, since it does require careful viewing and discussion. The film shows a short dramatic scene of three people for
whom drugs are simply a part of life, not a problem. The discussion
(which should last long but be difficult to begin) cues on words such
as freedom, responsibility, searching, love, drugs, life-style, loneliness,
life, death, boredom, and goals. *A Walk in the Park* does not provide
information, but it might just be the only really useful film in the
whole area of drug education.
(18 min., color, KING)

FILMSTRIPS

Guidance Associates has a number of filmstrips on various aspects of the drug problem. They have a series on teaching preventive drug education in elementary and secondary classrooms that is aimed specifically at teachers. In general their filmstrips are well-made, accurate, and interesting. Write them for a complete listing at Pleasantville, N.Y. 10570.

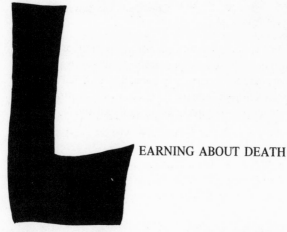

EARNING ABOUT DEATH

They think they're so smart giving the kids garbage like *Johnny Tremain* and *Giants of the Earth* and *Macbeth,* but do you know, I don't think there's a single kid in the whole joint who would know what to do if somebody dropped dead.

Paul Zindel, *The Pigman*

Every day 5,000 Americans do it. Die, that is. If the death is a "natural" one (usually meaning slow, smelly, and painful), there is a two-by-two-inch obituary written by a frustrated novelist often working, appropriately enough, on the graveyard shift. If the death is "unnatural" (usually meaning caused by a machine of some sort), the victim often receives a larger notice. If the corpse once owned an unusually large amount of money, his write-up is even larger.

His friends light candles, sing songs, shed tears, sprinkle water on the corpse and themselves, pay the undertaker, and go back to their daily routine of avoiding the same fate. They huddle together in crowds; they perform rituals, have babies, build monuments, madly scribble their own version of "Kilroy was here," pay life-insurance installments, and during breakfast read every gory detail of the latest mass murder. As Kurt Vonnegut would say, "So it goes."

If all the people who ever lived on the face of the planet earth would return from the dead, we the survivors would be outnumbered thirty to one. If each of our thirty ghosts came to America, they would notice in those still alive an almost obsessive fear of the experience called death. They would notice a repression of thoughts, of scientific study, and of feelings about the one event that is inevitable for man.

Arnold Toynbee has called death "un-American," and J. B. Priestley claims "mankind is frightened by the mere word 'death' and nowhere more so than in America." The thirty ghosts would see death hidden from children, the dying isolated from the living, and the schools teaching how to play basketball, solve quadratic equations, and learn who the vice-president in 1898 was. But they would never see the living young learn how to die or even how to live with the certainty of death. So it goes.

Much of our culture is a response, however inadequate, to the fear of death. This fear is an active motivation force among all people, including those young enough to be studying in a high school and those old enough to be teaching. Perhaps we the living sense that 10,000 irreplaceable nerve cells die each day. Perhaps we instinctively realize what it took Dr. Nathan Shock ten years of research to discover: namely that almost all bodily functions start declining around age eighteen to twenty. At thirty they begin deteriorating at a faster rate, which remains constant until death. In plain language, we go over the hill at twenty, and the downgrade steepens after thirty. Much of what we do in the name of teaching, art, creativity, and work is a secret but desperate attempt to avoid the inevitable decline.

"Death is the most important question of our time," according to psychohistorian Robert Jay Lifton. It might be at the root of more of our problems than we suspect. At one of the first New York radical bombings the explanatory letter claimed that "In death-directed Amerika, there is only one way to a life of love and freedom: to attack and destroy the forces of death." And the founding document of the now all but defunct SDS, the Port Huron Statement, was forged under the stark realization that "we may be the last generation in the experiment with living."

In spite of death's universality and power, science has rarely challenged the belief that death is not a phenomenon which can be subjected to scientific study. The doubling of the bibliography relating to death in the past few years is proof that scientists are now just beginning to realize the value of death study.

A THEORY

I have a pet theory that goes something like this: what a particular culture considers obscene reveals its most threatening fear. Obscenity is a social way of enforcing a taboo, of keeping a subject away from the dinner table. Death is becoming the new obscenity.

Our attitude toward death is to deny and brand as taboo rather than confront. Dr. Rollo May, writing in *Love and Will*, says, "The ways we repress death and its symbolism are amazingly like the ways the Victorians repressed sex. . . . Death is not talked of in front of the children, nor talked about at all if we can help it."

In the Middle Ages, when Church history *was* history, the most obscene comment one could make was antireligious in character. Many of these religious obscenities or profanities still exist today, but are not as shocking or blasphemous as they were in the religion-saturated Middle Ages. Expressions such as *damn* and *hell* can even appear in popular education magazines today without raising the proverbial eyebrow. An innocent expression such as *holy mackerel* is little heard today and would cause no shock if used in public. However, in Medieval France it was an accusation of being God's whore. *Bloody* as used by the English in "a bloody good show" dates back to a contraction of the expression *By Our Lady,* referring to the Virgin Mary. *Hocus Pocus* is another term now harmless which was once a sacrilegious blasphemy. The phrase is a corruption of the Latin word of consecration used in a Catholic Mass. *Gee* and *gads* were once vulgar references to God and Christ but are now common interjections.

Once religion began to lose its hold, hell, damnation, and blessed virginity became less frightening or awe-inspiring and have today all but lost their shock value.

Today almost anyone, when asked to think of a list of three "dirty" words, 99.9 percent of the time will choose words relating to sex and the body. We have met the enemy and they are we; our greatest fear is our body and its enjoyment.

But from Esalen to *Oh! Calcutta!* we are rediscovering the body. Concomitant with this rediscovery of the body, four-letter sex and body words are finding their ways into higher levels of respectability. Eventually these words might assume the mild taboos we today attach to the religious profanities of the Middle Ages.

As values change, a new obscenity will become socially unacceptable. The new obscenity will be death.

Already we see signs of certain death words surrounded with an aura of bluntness or impropriety. *Cemeteries* have turned into *gardens;* *graves* have given way to *plots* or *resting places; corpses* (perish the word) are not *buried* but *interred* or *laid to rest.* And people *pass away* instead of just plain *dying.* Try talking about death at the dinner table some time and decide if a bit of the taboo hasn't already descended.

Having overcome our fear of the wrath of God, having at least begun to learn to enjoy our bodies, we are still afraid of the unknown we call death.

IN THE CLASSROOM

One of the most consistent themes in student films and creative writing is death. It is usually a felt concern rather than an intellectual one. Any serious study of death in a high school classroom should be both intellectual (theories of when and why death occurs, afterlife, body disposal, the American way of death, attitudes toward death, etc.) and emotional (what do you feel about death and afterlife? what does this fear make you do? when do you think about death? etc.).

It should also in some way be experiential. Novelist Jerzy Kosinski taught a seminar at Yale called Death and the American Imagination. The course was to deal with all facets of death as it has expressed itself historically, philosophically, and in literature in the American experience. He too realized that such a course should be experiential; he also realized that only a dozen or so students could be accepted for the seminar, and the lecture hall was packed on the first class with potential students. He pointed out to the overflow crowd that the seminar would have to confront the experience of death firsthand, that they would first visit places of death and dying, and perhaps torture and kill a few small animals. "Regrettably," he added in a scholarly tone, "in order for the experience to be complete, it will be necessary for one member of the seminar to die." Enough took his ironic put-on seriously to solve the problem of class size.

The history, science, and sociology of death all deserve study and have all been swept under the curriculum carpet in favor of more "weighty" matters. In literature death plays a constant role (name five books or movies in which no one dies) but is rarely dealt with in class discussion. In school, as in the rest of culture, death is hidden and made painless to us survivors.

The questions and suggestions for classroom study which follow really deserve mature thought, discussion, and study. They are offered here simply in the hope that someone will be able to put them to use.

Questions on the Social Level

Is the attitude of Americans toward death substantially different from the attitude of Europeans, Africans, or Asians?

How is death viewed and dealt with in other cultures?

What are some primitive ideas of death?

What are the various answers to the question "What happens to people after death?"

Describe a society in which no one has to die unless he wishes.

Suicide: should it be a right? (Suicide ranks tenth in leading causes of death in the U.S. and if properly reported, might rank as high as fifth. There are twice as many suicides as homicides in the U.S. Suicide victims include: Jack London, Ernest Hemingway, Sara Teasdale, Vachel Lindsay, Hart Crane, Edgar Allan Poe, Marilyn Monroe, James Forrestal, Virginia Woolf, Vincent Van Gogh. Suicide is fifth in frequency as a cause of death among fifteen- to nineteen-year-olds.)

Investigate Cryonics. (See Bibliography under Life Extension Society, page 134.)

If you had to design a perfect funeral, what would it be like?

What could be done with bodies after death? If burial is continued, will we eventually run out of valuable space?

How is death presented in popular music?

Is death presented differently in movies now than it used to be?

How can society better prepare its members for death?

Investigate the donation of the body to science.

How serious is the possibility of global death from atomic warfare or the collapse of the ecosystem?

Do people ever have the right to cause the death of others?

How does advertising exploit the fear of death?

Death is the new obscenity.

Agree or disagree with this statement of Freud's: "In the unconscious everyone of us is convinced of his own immortality."

Take a poll of the school or class, and compare your results with the

Gallup poll which showed that "one out of every four people who believe in God do not believe in a resurrection."

On a personal level
How do you feel about your own death?
What experience have you had with death so far?
What is the closest you have ever come to dying? How do you feel about it?
What will happen to you after you die?
How would you like to die and when?
Describe your own funeral.
Do you have a right to take your own life?
What do you believe will happen to you after you die?
How does this belief influence your daily actions?
What would you do if you were immune from death?
It has been said that life is not worth living if there is nothing for which one is willing to die. Is there anything for which you would give your life?
Have you ever considered suicide? (Eighty percent of people in surveys admit to having "played" with the idea.)
Would you donate your body to science?
What would you like said about yourself in your obituary?
What do you do to postpone death? What are you currently doing or not doing because of fear of death?
What would you do if you were told you had a month to live?
What words in common use are related to death? (E.g., bury, dead, deadly)

Activities and Death Experiences
Visit a place or places of death as a group. For a start try any of the following: county morgue, funeral parlor (behind the scenes), cemetery (especially an old one), church funeral of a stranger, suicide prevention center.
Doctors or nurses are usually invited to schools to speak about health or sex; yet they are exposed to more dying than almost any other occupational group. Have a nurse or doctor tell about their experiences with death and how they treat a person they know is dying. Do they tell the person or do they tell only his relatives? How do people die? How do others act when people die? Does it hurt to die?

Conduct a group fantasy: attend your own funeral. For this fantasy the leader should pace the direction comments, so individuals have time to concoct fantasies that are credible. Participants should have some familiarity with fantasizing from previous experiences. The following instructions are given from the fantasy leader's viewpoint and constitute a kind of script he could use in guiding the group.

Lie down on your back, placing your hands at your sides.

Imagine your life has left you. Close your eyes, do not move or speak.

You are in a funeral parlor and people are coming to see you.

Look at the faces of the people above you.

Who is there?

How are they feeling? What does each one say?

Is there someone there who is glad you are dead?

Is there someone there who envies your being dead?

Select some of the people who come to see you and say something to them. (This is done silently, of course.) In other words, if you could speak to people for one last time and had absolutely nothing to fear from them, what would you say?

Involve at least one other person in this group in your funeral.

Someone is giving your eulogy; what is he saying? What would you like him to say?

Prepare, discuss, and tabulate a questionnaire on death. Have students administer the questionnaire both to themselves and to their parents, other relatives, and friends. Such an approach will often provoke discussion between teens and parents about death and sometimes open lines of communication that have been long closed. Be prepared as a teacher, however, to be accused of doing "morbid" things which have little to do with education. A classroom study of death can be more controversial than sex education in a conservative suburb.

Class involvement in preparing a questionnaire is educational in itself. A good source for the questionnaire is the August 1970 issue of *Psychology Today* which contains a reader questionnaire, "You and Death"; the results appeared in the June 1971 issue. A few suggestions for the questionnaire items follow:

When you were a child, how was death talked about in your family? (a) Openly; (b) with some sense of discomfort; (c) only when necessary and then with an attempt to exclude the children; (d) as though it were a forbidden topic; (e) don't recall any discussion of death.

To the best of your memory, at what age were you first aware of death?

(a) Under three; (b) three to five; (c) five to ten; (d) ten or older.

Other questions could include queries about the extent of belief in a life after death, personal wishes about life after death, the meaning of death, the aspect of death that is most distasteful, feelings about one's own death, length of life desired, preferred method of death, willingness to die for some cause, suicide, wishes about use of body after death, etc.

IDEAS FOR DISCUSSION, RESEARCH, OR CONTEMPLATION

Our lives are poisoned by a fear of death, and much of our culture represents a response, however inadequate, to this fear. . . . Insofar as we consider the possibility of our own death at all, it is as an event that is as remote as the end of time, and so we tend unconsciously to repress the fear and the fact of our ultimate doom, or consciously to forget it.

Living with the constant fear of death, rather than just the awareness of death, contaminates life and adversely affects man's capacity to enjoy it. It is difficult, if not impossible, to live spontaneously and positively with joy if we are constantly fearful of losing all we have and are haunted with a sense of futility about all existence (*Overcoming the Fear of Death* by David Gordon [New York: Macmillan, 1970]).

Aging begins when growth stops, around 18-20. Almost all functions then start declining slowly. At 30 they begin deteriorating at a faster but still modest rate which remains constant until death. In plain language, we go over the hill at 20, and the downgrade steepens after 30. We lose weight; reaction times slow; we cannot take as big breaths; our strength ebbs; we cannot work as hard. Even the ability to enjoy the world diminishes as hearing fails and taste buds stop functioning ("Aging: The Disease With a Cure," by Bruce Frish, *Science Digest,* February 1969).

Often the job of informing the patient of his coming demise is turned over to the nursing staff; at other times patients, hospital staff and relatives all indulge in a grim pretense that death is not imminent. One survey among dying patients revealed that 80 percent of them believed that they should be told their prognosis, while 80 percent of their doctors believed that the truth should be withheld ("The Psychology of Death," *Newsweek,* 14 September 1970).

There is almost no relationship between what people think they think about death and how they really feel when faced with it (Robert Kastenbaum, psychologist).

Sports such as skiing and auto-racing break through to the illusion of immortality by means of speed. Skating, sailing, riding the surf, skin and sky-diving take us out of ourselves so that we become temporarily death-free. We escape death by dancing, moving into a new kind of time based on variations of our heart beat. . . . The narcotic drift will take you to space beyond time and death, as well as an orgy or a church organ (*The Immortalist* by Alan Harrington [New York: Random House, 1969]).

When an individual begins to die, much of what he suffers is the result of the fear of death on his own part and on the part of those around him. He reminds people that they too are going to die, which they naturally are not eager to consider.

Doctors apparently shy from the subject because death represents a defeat and because, like everybody else, they find death upsetting to talk about. . . . Doctors generally end by suppressing awareness of death so thoroughly some researchers speculate that that is why they are drawn to medicine in the first place.

There is a . . . characteristic return of the dying to infancy. Gradually they sleep longer each day, until they wake for only minutes at a time. Emotionally, the dying become increasingly dependent. Waking in the night they may cry if they discover they are alone, or sink back to sleep if someone is there ("Learning To Die" by Thomas Powers, *Harper's,* June 1971).

Thus that which is the most awful of evils, death, is nothing to us, since when we exist there is not death, and when there is death we do not exist (Epicurus).

The goal of all life is death (Sigmund Freud).

A single death is a tragedy; a million deaths is a statistic (Joseph Stalin).

Most people are no longer alive after their entrance into maturity. They commit a partial and token suicide by stopping their growth and stopping the pleasure of expansion. They bury themselves in old accepted habits and customs, drowning their sense of curiosity regarding new inner and outer experiences. Contented apathy and the ending of inquisitive curiosity may be looked at as the early intrusion of death.

In our mourning and in our homage to the dead, we cleanse ourselves partly of eventual earlier hostile wishes toward the deceased person or toward those they may have represented. A bitter philosopher expressed this in a cynical play on words by saying about the cemetery: Here lie the dead and here lie the living.

We have to realize that there usually exists more dread of life than fear of death. Life for people who attempt suicide is the greater insecurity, while death holds out the promise of peace (*Suicide and Mass Suicide* by J. A. Meerloo [New York: Dutton, 1968]).

When actress Marilyn Monroe surrendered to the torments of her life in August, 1962, and died through an overdose of sleeping drugs, a wave of suicides followed in her wake all over the world. In the ensuing days the death rate through suicide in New York and Chicago rose to five times the usual average (*Journal of the American Medical Association*, 6 October 1964).

ADDITIONAL TEACHER-STUDENT BIBLIOGRAPHY

The American Way of Death by Jessica Mitford (New York: Fawcett World, 1969, $.95). A modern classic on the hypocrisy of funerals. Chapter titles include: Funeral Costs, The Story of Service (how the body is prepared to look "natural" and "life-like"), God's Little Million-Dollar Acre, Cremation, Fashion in Funerals, and The Allied Industries (undertakers, cemeteries, florists, monument makers, vault manufacturers). Jessica Mitford was singled out recently by a House Investigative Committee (alias House Un-American Activities) as one of 65 people that colleges and universities should consider subversive. Other "subversive" characters on the list included Nat Hentoff, John Ciardi, and Dr. Spock.

The Book: On the Taboo Against Knowing Who You Are by Alan Watts (New York: Collier, 1967; paperback, $.95). I've never tried this book with students but would guess that it could become as popular as *The Art of Loving.* The 150-page book is Watts' attempt to pass along to the future what is most important, what he calls "a new experience of what it is to be I."

Death Be Not Proud, a Memoir by John Gunther (New York: Harper & Row, 1949; paperback, $.60). A book that teens find especially moving. Gunther recounts his brilliant 17-year-old son's cheerful battle with a brain tumor and death. No one admitted the nearness of death to the boy; only afterward did his parents recognize that he did indeed know, but pretended that he didn't to spare them in return. It also shows parents' acceptance of the loss of a child: "I did not feel that God had personally singled out either him or us for any special act, either of animosity or generosity. In a way I did not feel that God was involved at all."

Destiny by Jeffrey Schrank (Morristown, N.J.: Silver Burdett, 1970, $.54 for 60-page illustrated paperback). I can't be too objective about this one, but I can say that the book is a discussion text dealing with the question, "Where am I going?" Brief chapters on artificial life, population, death by war, poems on death, aging, the dying, suicide, and autos.

Life Extension Society, 2011 N St., N.W., Washington, D.C. 20036, is the national society promoting the freezing of people as soon as they die in the hopes that science will determine how to unfreeze them at some future date. Their newsletter is titled "Freeze-Wait-Reanimate" and costs $2 a year or $1 for students. There are already a fair number of corpses existing in the frozen state. The cryogenic storage container costs $5,000 and the monthly charge for maintenance is about $50.

Books on the topic include *We Froze the First Man* by Robert Nelson (New York: Dell, 1968, $.75), an account of an actual cryonic freezing, and *The Prospect of Immortality* by Robert C. W. Ettinger, considered the founder of the cryonic movement (New York: Macfadden, 1969).

A Manual of Simple Burial by Ernest Morgan (Burnsville, N.C.: Cello Press; $1) is a 64-page guide to obtaining "simplicity, dignity, and economy in funeral arrangements through advance planning."

The booklet gives methods people can use to avoid the artificiality and stupidity of funeral homes. The manual's main suggestion for avoiding the undertaker is through membership in a memorial society. The manual lists addresses of such societies and provides information on cremation, autopsies, eye banks, bequeathal of bodies, and the business and legal aspects of death in America. There are also chapters on Interpreting Death To a Child and even What To Do When Death Occurs.

The Meaning of Death, Herman Feifel, ed. (New York: McGraw-Hill, 1959). An anthology of articles on death including authors such as Carl Jung, Paul Tillich, and Herbert Marcuse. Chapter titles include: The Child's View of Death, Time and Death in Adolescence, Mortality and Modern Literature, and Modern Art and Death.

Mixed Bag by Helene Hutchinson (Glenview, Ill.: Scott Foresman, 1970; $5.95). The author describes the book's purpose as "to excite interest and elicit emotional response by bringing into the classroom the colors and forms of the outside world." Included are ads, buttons, cartoons, photos, paintings, graffiti, song lyrics, poems, stories, and essays. Besides death, themes include family, violence, race, and religion.

National Kidney Foundation, 315 Park Ave. S., New York, N.Y., will send information on leaving parts of your body (kidney, eyes, heart, and others) for transplant purposes. Write for details.

The Pigman by Paul Zindel (New York: Dell, 1968) is one of the best novels available for reading and discussion among teen-agers. There are few books that are enjoyed by almost every student as readily as is *The Pigman.* The novel is well written and produces many misty eyes and faraway looks among readers. The story is about two teen-agers, John and Lorraine; the pervasive theme of the novel is death. Lorraine's mother heartlessly steals from and cares for terminal-cancer patients and receives special referral rates when she recommends a funeral home at the propitious moment. John's father won't survive his death-in-life job much longer and is anxious that John go into business with him. The Pigman only survives the loneliness after his wife's death through friendship with a baboon, and when the baboon dies, the Pigman can no longer live. John searches for the meaning of life and death in all these experiences; he often visits graveyards, explaining, "I think that's probably the real reason I go into the graveyard. I'm not afraid of seeing ghosts. I think I'm really looking for ghosts. I want to see them. I'm looking for anything to prove that when I drop dead there's a chance I'll be doing something a little more exciting than decaying."

Psychology Today, November 1970, contains an interview with Robert Jay Lifton. Lifton sees the danger of atomic annihilation as destroying man's hope for immortality. "I would say that the drug revolution, acid-rock music, the demand for turned-on social and political activities—these are all efforts to regain a collective sense of immortality. Woodstock and other youth festivals brought all of these elements together in a communal high, which is what community formation is all about.

DEATH IN CURRENT MUSIC

Rock and folk rock music has consistently been concerned with death. The Shangri-La's "Leader of the Pack," Mark Denning's "Teen Angel," Eddie Cochran's "Teenage Heaven," Bobby Gentry's "Ode to Billie Joe," Bobby Goldsboro's "Honey," The Band's "Long Black Veil," the Rolling Stones' "Paint It Black," Billy Edd Wheeler's "Winter Sky" (done by Judy Collins on *Recollections* album), Laura Nyro's "And When I Die" done by Blood, Sweat and Tears, George Harrison's "The Art of Dying" (on his *All Things Must Pass* album) and Procul Harum's album *Home* (the album's central theme is death and includes "About to Die," "The Dead Man's Dream," and "Nothing That I Didn't Know") —these are all directly concerned with death.

The rock addicts in any class can probably come up with other examples by the dozens. An interesting study and report would be on how rock music handles the theme of death.

FEATURE FILMS–A COMMENT

Consider *Bonnie and Clyde, Elvira Madigan, Butch Cassidy, Easy Rider, The Wild Bunch, If, Weekend, Love Story, Medium Cool, Romeo and Juliet,* and *Zabriskie Point.* They all end with dead heroes. It's not that all movies now have dead heroes; it's just that the biggest hits with the young crowd do.

Ten years ago the hero never died. But now the Happy Ending has had it. Since this trend took hold only since the killing of the Kennedys and King, one is tempted to speculate that it is once again an example of art imitating life. Heroes can die now, and they do. So it goes.

SHORT FILMS ABOUT DEATH

Chickamauga

In Robert Heinlein's science-fiction novel *The Moon Is a Harsh Mistress*, one of the characters says "Children seldom are able to realize that death will come to them personally. One might define adulthood as the age at which a person learns that he must die . . . and accepts his sentence undismayed." In *Chickamauga* a child begins to grow up. A deaf boy confronts so much death among the defeated army that it is incomprehensible. The dying soldiers are just another wonderful group of playmates or circus animals. He is able to cope with the unimaginable suffering around him through his childish fantasy. When he returns home the death of his mother does not register to him as death—how could he possibly understand what death means? His mother looks at him wide-eyed and unblinking; he cannot understand. He has inherited war and death as well as deafness.

(33 min., b&w, CF, Pyramid)

Corrida Interdite

Corrida Interdite is composed entirely of slow-motion shots from bull-fights accompanied by classical organ music. The film tells no story except that of the conflict between man and animal which, in reality, is one between man and man. Some of the shots of the bullfighters being gored produce strong feelings in the audience. Surprisingly, students often seem to cheer the bull when he gets the best of his human adversary. Once again a film useful for the reactions it produces.

(10 min., color, Pyramid, CFS)

The Day Grandpa Died

A 10-year-old Jewish boy arrives home from school one day to find his grandfather has died. His parents try to help him cope with this loss. His mother reminds him that grandpa was seventy-three and had a good, full life while his father tells him "You lost a grandfather; I lost a father."

Through flashbacks the viewer is shown the warm relationship that existed between the boy and his grandfather. There is a burial scene where the rabbi observes that "people don't die as long as we keep them in our memory; people only die when we forget them." Nature imagery of the boy and grandfather planting a small tree and of a leafless tree against a blue sky are used to suggest that death is more than an end.

The film is a well-made and sensitive treatment of a boy's reaction to the death of his grandpa. It is useful in eliciting discussion and feelings from children about death.

(12 min., color, King)

The Day Manolete Was Killed

The Day Manolete Was Killed and *Corrida Interdite,* which is described above, are two effective classroom films about bullfighting. *The Day Manolete Was Killed* is not a well-made film, but it does succeed in telling the true story of a dead hero. It shows Manolete's rise to fame and his desire to give himself to the fans. He retired healthy and rich, but came out of retirement to defend his reputation against a flashy newcomer. In August, 1947, a multimillionaire and a bull killed each other. We admire dead heroes. Manolete is no exception. Excellent for producing feelings and discussion.

(19 min., b&w, EB, FI, UC, UM)

Death

This film, without morbidity, reveals how carefully society avoids the subject of death and how ill-prepared most of us are for the terror and isolation of that last severance. The camera follows one man, Albro Pearsall, a 52-year-old terminal-cancer patient, through his last days at Calvary Hospital in the Bronx. This is both a personal portrait of a man who faces death without deception and a study of the responses of a family, doctors, nurses, hospital attendants, and other patients to the dying person. Doctors discuss the psychology of dying and the manner used with the dying patient. Nurses' aides are trained to accept the fact that they must be satisfied with their limited ability to give comfort and ease pain. The film discusses the difficulty in communicating with the dying person, the psychological defenses used by the patient and whether they help or betray him in his last moments, and the part religion plays. In a broader sense, the film is a deeply affecting reminder of our own mortality and the need to live fully. "You can't start really living," says one doctor in the film, "unless you've personally solved the problem of your dying."

(42 min., b&w, UC, UM, PSU)

La Jette
La Jette is the unlikely combination of science-fiction and a love story. The scene is the jetty of Paris' Orly airport a few years before World War III. A small boy sees a man die. He is lucky enough to be one of the survivors of the war who is taken prisoner and selected for experiments. The victors choose him to travel into the past and the future. In so doing he understands that the man he once witnessed being shot at Orly was himself, grown up.

The film was made by Chris Marker in France and is narrated, with English subtitles. The highly visual film has won international awards. It could be discussed as science fiction, as cinematic art, as a piece of literature, or for the ideas it presents. In a unit on death, film works especially well with more mature students to explore the cyclic concept of time and feelings about one's own death.
(27 min., b&w, Pyramid)

The Mood of Zen and *Man, Nature and Zen Buddhism*
Briefly, these are nature collages with narration by Alan Watts. Watts presents some of the Eastern ideas associated with Zen. The idea of death is different from that held by Westerners. From the narration: "Man and nature are one process . . . death is like the winter. We don't say 'there ought to be no winter.' No winter, no summer, no valleys without mountains, no life without death. Life is like music. We don't play it to get somewhere. It's a pattern which we listen to and enjoy as it unfolds. The best musicians aren't those who get to the end first."
(15 min. each, color, HARTLEY, MSU, PSU for *Mood of Zen* and HARTLEY, PSU, MMM for *Man, Nature and Zen Buddhism*.

Nahanni
No one dies in *Nahanni*. A 73-year-old, gutsy prospector challenges the hostile Nahanni River in Canada's Northwest territory and loses for the eighth time. The river has claimed other lives but the old man vows to try again and not to stop until he dies. The film is useful to introduce the ideas of Robert Jay Lifton and Alan Harrington, which attribute much of man's activity to the motivation of achieving immortality.
(19 min., color, CF)

Occurrence at Owl Creek Bridge
If we did not fear death *Occurrence at Owl Creek Bridge* would not be the classic it is. It is our fear of death which causes us to identify with the man about to be hanged and to overlook the visual clues which tell quite plainly that the film is a dream. The whole film is about how it feels to be "a livin' man." Why couldn't this heightened consciousness of life be ours as a normal thing? Why does it take an imminent death to bring it forth? An excellent film for dealing with death and feelings.
(27 min., b&w, CF, FSU, SUNYB, Pyramid, CU, ROA, UC, NU, UU)

Omega
Omega is the *2001* of the short film. The film is about the death and rebirth of man, his evolutionary transcendence into something infra-human. The film is more of a trip or visual experience than a story film. *Omega's* special effects won Donald Fox the award for best experimental short at the Chicago Film Festival and also won an award at the Atlanta film festival. *Omega* is more of an experience than a mere discussion starter, and the experience of watching it can certainly be used to explore the outer limits of ideas about death, evolution, the afterlife, and the future of mankind.
(13 min., color, Pyramid)

The Red Kite
A man buys a red kite to fly with his little girl. On the bus on the way home from work on Friday he overhears a comment while passing a cemetery that "when a person dies that's the end—that's all there is—it's all a sham."

He is troubled by the remark, and it brings to the surface his own lack of confidence and repressed fear of death. The red kite is a symbol for man's overcoming the grave as it soars above a cemetery on an Autumn Sunday morning. The juxtaposition of autumn, Sunday morning, and the red kite is a well-chosen symbolic triad.

The film is not the most involving one available for high school students, but it does deal with death symbolism and the indirect effects of the fear of death.
(20 min., color, CF, UM, ROA)

The Summer We Moved to Elm Street
The Summer We Moved to Elm Street is a NFBC production about a
family headed by an alcoholic father. The McGraw-Hill Contemporary
catalog subtitled the film "alcoholism" but in my mind it has always
been more about death than drink.

A little girl confronts an apparent death for the first time. She tries
to grapple with the fact that whatever has been given to her was later
taken back. In a childlike way she wonders if this is true of life itself.
Like Steinbeck's *The Red Pony* this film is about the initiation into
the fact of death. As the film ends the family moves again, to yet another street to begin again.
(28 min., color, CF, MMM, UM, PSU, ROA)

When Angels Fall
When Angels Fall will either be a powerful emotional experience or
one of the most ridiculous films seen. With a very young or immature
audience the latter is the most likely reaction.

A Roman Polanski short made in 1958, it tells the story of an aged
lady who cleans a public lavatory and watches over it during the day.
As she watches she thinks back to the days of the past when she was
young and sensuous. Her past is filled with passion and sorrow, her
present with a lavatory and memories.

As she sits alone in the evening an angel crashes through the sky-
light. Her lover has returned. The ending sounds ridiculous, but taken
in the context of the film is surprisingly powerful.

The value of this film in a study of death is in its presentation of
old age. The flashbacks show the aged lady when she was young and
beautiful by our standards. Rarely do students picture themselves as
old. After seeing *When Angels Fall*, they can hardly help but consider
age and death.
(21 min., color, CF)

UBVERSIVE ACTIVITIES

*Being Classroom Experiences
to Promote Unlearning*

INVISIBLE WALLS

Topic: Body language.
Purpose: To create greater awareness of the role of body language.
Each of us carries around a private bubble which extends all around us
for about eighteen inches. This bubble contains what we like to consider personal space.

We consider any stranger's invasion of this personal space as an af-
front, perhaps even an attack. It is a space we have learned from our
culture to create. We allow people into this personal area only when we
cannot avoid it (crowded elevators or buildings), when that person has
some special function (tailor, doctor), or when we agree that a state of
intimacy exists (husband-wife, children).

This invisible bubble can be demonstrated by setting up interviews
in the front of the classroom. The student conducting the interview
should be aware of the experiment, but the class should be led to believe that the interviews are being conducted only because the topic is
important. The interviewer should be armed with a notebook for jotting
down notes and should actually ask a series of well-prepared questions.
As he does so, he should step very close to the person being interviewed,
"pushing" into his personal space. This invasion should be done very
slowly but definitely. If the interviewee moves back, the interviewer
should pursue until the short interview is finished.

After a number of people have been questioned and "invaded," ask those interviewed about their feelings while being questioned. They all will have signaled by their body movement that they were uncomfortable; the test is whether they were aware of this feeling and can tell where it came from. See if they can recognize how they "defended" themselves against the questioner's invasion of their personal space. Many will have used a stance at right angle to the questioner; others will have constantly stared out into space without even looking at the interviewer; others will have slowly backed away and taken another position.

Once the whole class is aware of the phenomenon of personal space, try an interview with an unsuspecting outsider, maybe the principal. Have students experiment with personal space in public, show the film *Invisible Walls* (described on page 25), or discuss sections from Julius Fast's *Body Language* (page 19) or Edward T. Hall's *The Silent Language* (see page 21).

WORDLESS CONVERSATION

Topic: Nonverbal communication; body language.
*Purpose: To introduce the fact that people communicate constantly
          without words.*
Select three to five volunteers and send them out of the room. Do not tell them what they will have to do. While they are out of hearing, explain to the group that the volunteers will be asked to carry on a three-minute conversation without using words, sounds, or props. They are to remain seated during the whole time.

The remainder of the group will be observers, watching for what the volunteers communicate through their body language. Observers will watch for signs of embarrassment, feelings of responsibility for the conversation, awkwardness, leadership, confidence or lack of confidence, nervousness, etc.

Call the volunteers back in the room, and direct them to carry on the three-minute nonverbal conversation. Do not explain what the rest of the group will be watching for.

After the three minutes (which will seem like thirty to the volunteers), discuss what the volunteers communicated to the rest of the group. Encourage the volunteers to talk about the feelings they had during the three minutes.

This exercise serves as a fine introduction to the topic of body language.

EYES

Topic: Eye contact.
Purpose: To demonstrate the dynamics of eye contact and to examine one's own use of eye contact.

In our culture we are taught that when passing a person on the street, an eye contact of only about a second is permissible. Anything longer becomes threatening or could be interpreted as sexual.

Eyes do speak. Alexander Lowen in *Betrayal of the Body* writes that "more than any other single sign, the expression in the eyes of a person indicates to what extent he is in 'possession of his faculties.'" In his view a common denominator among persons suffering from schizophrenia is that they are unable to focus their eyes with feeling upon another person.

Behavioral scientists claim that a single glance is all that is necessary between two people to tell who is most likely to dominate the relationship. Most often the person who averts his eyes first signals to the other that he is about to claim the floor—that he is dominant. The scientists claim 80 percent success in predicting on the basis of first eye contact dominance and submission between two people.

In our society we don't stare at people, only at nonpersons. Enemies, athletes and performers, servants, and objects are OK to stare at, but not friends or strangers. In meeting someone while passing along the sidewalk the usual pattern is to look at the person until he is about eight feet away, then to look away as he passes. We really have rather rigid rules about eye contact that we follow in public places. Discuss what the commonly agreed rules about eye contact are when one is in an elevator or a crowded bus, or carrying on an interview or a normal conversation.

Or try this: have each person pick a partner at random, and have the partners stare into each other's eyes for as long as possible. Then discuss the feelings during that time, the reasons it was difficult or embarrassing, or why giggles broke out so soon, etc. Deal with possible feelings of superiority, masculinity, embarrassment, or enjoyment.

Try cutting out the eyes in pictures of public figures in newspapers or magazines. Have the group tell as much as they can about the person, judging solely by the eyes. Identify the person only after the group has discussed what they see in the eyes.

Have the group examine their own eye behavior and that of others for one week and report back. Have them try some experiments with eye contact.

Further References

Read chapter 9 of Julius Fast's *Body Language* or Erving Goffman's *Interaction Ritual* or *Behavior in Public Places*. There are also excellent sections in Sandor Feldman's *Mannerisms of Speech and Gestures in Everyday Life*. (All four books are in paperback.)

DID YOU HEAR WHAT I HEAR?

Topic: Listening.
Purpose: To demonstrate the concentration needed to participate in a group discussion and to give practice in listening and understanding to other group members.

This is a technique that helps improve group discussions; it is best introduced when a group shows signs of a communication breakdown or argumentative stall.

It is simple to describe but surprisingly hard to put into action. Each person who speaks in the group must summarize what the person who spoke immediately before him said, to that person's satisfaction. Only after he has done so may he make his own contribution.

The technique helps group members realize that they often spend much time thinking of what they want to say rather than listening to what others are saying. The exercise also helps others realize the amount of "reading into" others' remarks they do. The technique slows down a group and makes the discussion proceed at what seems like an artificial pace, but it does help people become more conscious of listening.

PASSING A RUMOR

Topic: Communication distortion.
Purpose: To analyze and demonstrate the communication distortion that occurs even when an honest attempt is made to communicate accurately and sincerely.

Groups divide into sixes for this experiment. One person in each group is given a written story of about a hundred words—something like an accident report, a movie plot, or a description of a thief. This person reads the story in a whisper to the person on his left. That person whispers as best he can the story to the next person. The third person tells it to the fourth, and so on until the last person in each group is told the story. The last person tells his version of the story to the whole group. The original should then be read to everyone, and the process of how the story became distorted should be analyzed.

Discussion should center on why distortion occurred; rare is the group that fails to change the story drastically. To help the discussion, a tape recorder could be used to record the different versions of the description.

MEDITATION ON ME

Topic: Self-image.
Purpose: To think about oneself, make a self-description, clarify one's self-image, and determine what in that image is most valued.

Before the activity, see that each student has eight small pieces of paper. Students should close their eyes, become comfortable, and let their minds play with words and phrases that describe themselves. Allow at least five minutes of quiet for this to happen. As in many of the experiences described here, the teacher should act as a participant in the activity.

When the group seems finished, have them open their eyes and write on the eight pieces of paper the words and phrases that came to mind during the self-meditation. Tell them that these pieces of paper will not be for anyone but themselves.

After the eight papers are filled, have students arrange them in order, putting the one they like best in the first position and the one they like least in the last. The other six should be ranked according to the degree of happiness or satisfaction they give.

Then have students spend some time with the word or phrase on each sheet of paper, fantasizing about it or recalling experiences they associate with the word. Caution them to take all the time they want with each word. Then encourage them to do whatever they wish with each piece of paper—throw it away, change it, give it to someone, or write on it.

After the experience the group can, if they are capable, share feelings during the exercise or do a written evaluation. An activity like this would be far less effective if performed out of context or simply to kill time or do something different. It is most effective in the context of a group or class where self-knowledge is recognized as a valid and deserved class activity.

A fifteen to eighteen session course titled "Developing the Potential of the Adolescent" is detailed in Dr. Hubert A. Otto's book *Group Methods to Actualize Human Potential* ($9.95 from National Center for the Exploration of Human Potential, 8080 El Paseo Grande, La Jolla, Calif. 92037).

PERSONALITY MIRROR

Topic: Self-concept.
Purpose: To compare one's view of self with the way others see him.
In this exercise group, members should not be complete strangers. Group size should be somewhere between eight and twenty per small group. The teacher or group leader should participate rather than act as director, if possible.

Enough copies of the Feedback Profile sheets should be given out, so that each person can mark a sheet for everyone in the group, himself included. In a group of ten, each person would receive ten Feedback Profile sheets.

Each person first fills out the profile for himself and then does the same for others in his group. These instructions should be announced before beginning:
1. The 0 and 8 choices should be considered extremes beyond which people really exist. Therefore only 1-7 are valid choices. The 0 and 8 may not be chosen.
2. One number should be circled on each continuum. Four represents the choice for a quality solidly between the two extremes.
3. Be fair, serious, and consistent about the selections.

4. No one will see the profile you mark for yourself.
5. After everyone is finished, each person will receive the profiles the others marked about him.

After the profiles have been completed and redistributed, provide each person with another profile sheet on which he can compute his average score for each category. Each person should figure his own averages and compare them to the profile he marked for himself.

Discussion afterwards should focus on the discrepancies between how each person sees himself and how others see him. If, for example, a person marked himself a 2 on the conformist-rebel scale and the group marked him a 5, the reason behind the difference should be explored.

Some people will have no discrepancies. For them the exercise serves as a confirmation that their self-concept is fairly realistic.

FEEDBACK PROFILE

Name _____

Physical Superman										Physical mouse
	0	1	2	3	4	5	6	7	8	
Extreme conservative										Extreme radical
	0	1	2	3	4	5	6	7	8	
Optimist										Pessimist
	0	1	2	3	4	5	6	7	8	
Dumbbell										Genius
	0	1	2	3	4	5	6	7	8	
Likes a large number of friends										Prefers a few close friends
	0	1	2	3	4	5	6	7	8	
Fantastically good-looking										Extremely ugly
	0	1	2	3	4	5	6	7	8	

Rational, intellectual, detached										Emotional, feeling, subjective

0   1   2   3   4   5   6   7   8

Instant friendship with everyone										Almost impossible to get to know

0   1   2   3   4   5   6   7   8

MOTIVE ANALYSIS
Topic: Motive projection.
Purpose: To examine the tendency to attribute one's own motives to the actions of others.

People often see themselves as doing some action for a noble cause. They see others doing the same thing for less lofty ideals. I might consider studying yoga because I believe it is a valid means of spiritual growth. But I see others studying yoga largely because it is hip or faddish.

Another tendency is to project onto others my own true motivation. So, for example, I am really studying yoga simply to be considered hip but refuse to admit this. I defend myself by projecting this motive onto others and attributing to myself more sincere reasons.

The questionnaire which follows demonstrates both these tendencies and can be used with a variety of topics. The questionnaire compares one's own reasons for some choice with those reasons one believes motivate others. Discussion centers on the difference between how I see my own motives and how I see others. The questionnaire also often reveals true motives that are rarely openly admitted.

This questionnaire was used in a high school where 99 percent of the students go on to college.

Rate each of the following motives for choosing a college according to this scale:

1. Does not apply at all
2. Applies only a little
3. Makes a fair amount of difference

4. A strong factor
5. A very strong factor

Rate each motive as it applies to you and as you think it applies to the others in the class.

Myself	*Others*	*Motive*
_____	_____	Status and prestige
_____	_____	Close to home
_____	_____	Far away from home
_____	_____	Easy to get into
_____	_____	Easy to get a degree from
_____	_____	Provides a high-quality education
_____	_____	Good athletic program
_____	_____	Good place to find a marriage partner
_____	_____	Good place to experiment with different life-styles
_____	_____	Easy sex
_____	_____	Friends are going there
_____	_____	Simply the closest school

After each person fills out the questionnaire the totals for each item should be compared. For example, "Provides a high-quality education" received a rating of 80 (group of 20) in the Myself column but only a 62 in the Others column. The figures were almost exactly reversed for "Status and prestige."

The direction of the discussion following the questionnaire is difficult to control, but it is always lively. The questionnaire often promotes discussion outside of scheduled school time and does help in questioning one's own motives.

Some other possible topics for motive analysis include attendance at church services, basis for choosing a career, and attitude toward military service.

DREAMS

Topic: Self-awareness.
Purpose: To regain contact with one's dreams.
We spend nearly one-third of our lives dreaming and are almost totally

cut off from this part of ourselves. Our culture teaches that dreams are not important and so we "forget" our dreams. The Egyptians considered dreams a portent of the future; the Greeks used dreams as a way of fighting disease; the Iroquois made important life decisions based on dreams; and Americans ignore them.

When one mentions dreams today, students immediately think of psychoanalysis (even though they don't use that particular word). We are not suggesting using dreams to analyze students or even to help them analyze themselves in either Jungian or Freudian terms. We do suggest that dreams are an important human operation that deserves conscious attention. We also believe that people can be taught to increase their ability to recall dreams and will thereby be more in touch with themselves than if dream matter were repressed.

Have students try to recall dreams and write them down. See if they can improve the number of dreams they can remember. The first myth to deal with is "I don't dream." Once students are aware of the fact that dreams can be remembered, many will be able to improve their dream recall considerably. As an introduction it would be good to present various theories about dreams.

SECRET WISHES

Topic: The roots of hatred.
Purpose: Confronting and accepting hidden feelings.
One common assumption which seems to be part of our culture is that an "acceptable" person does not have "unacceptable" desires. These "unacceptable" desires produce guilt feelings, not so much because of the desires themselves but because society disapproves of them. Actually, all people have desires that could be considered unacceptable.

If one does admit to desires which might be considered depraved or sadistic, others (concealing similar desires) react with shock. This disapproval produces self-doubts that tend to make a person alienate himself from these desires. Hiding the desires in turn produces guilt that becomes harmful. When projected on someone else, such guilt often comes out as prejudice or outrage.

For example, the outrage at youth's sexuality or "dirty movies" is often merely a secret desire for the same which a person refuses to admit and instead projects in the form of concern for the morals of the young.

When people become aware that "taboo" feelings are common to most people, they can start moving toward accepting and integrating them into their personality. The following technique is a relatively non-threatening procedure for dealing with such hidden feelings.

Provide a pencil and quarter sheets of paper for each person in the group. If the group is larger than ten, it should be divided into smaller groups which each have one person who is aware of the basis of the exercise. Some sort of professional training would probably be helpful for these leaders.

Group members are asked to write on the paper a secret, a taboo wish that they have. They are assured that they will never have to identify what they write. The papers should be folded, collected, and redistributed at random so each person has a secret other than his own.

Each person is then asked to assume that the secret on the paper is really his own. He should tell what it is like to have such a secret desire, and the group should try to help him reconcile the desire with his personality.

The main idea behind the sharing is that people realize that such desires are not unusual and that they experience an acceptance rather than a rejection of such feelings.

For further reference: *The Adjusted American: Normal Neuroses in the Individual and Society* by Snell Putney and Gail J. Putney (New York: Harper Colophon Book CN95, Harper & Row, 1964). Especially Chapter 4, "Mirror of Hatred."

ALL OR NOTHING

Topic: The values affecting decision making; the group process.
Purpose: To determine what values influence a difficult decision.
Select four to eight volunteers who are willing to pay twenty-five cents or more to take part in an experiment. If there is a dearth of volunteers (which is rare), tell the class there is a chance to make money from the experiment. Have the students form a circle while the remainder of the class watches. Collect the quarter from each volunteer.

Place the money in the center of the circle (for dramatic effect), and explain that in a given time limit (ten minutes is good) the group must decide who gets all the money. The money must all go to *one* person; no deals to split the money after the game are permitted. Appoint no group leader, and place no restriction on techniques.

Younger students take this game especially seriously and tend to become more involved than the money at stake seems to warrant. Usually groups decide on luck as the means of distribution. After the decision (the winner does keep the money, by the way) the entire class discusses the group process and the values that were demonstrated in making the decision. Why did the group choose luck as a problem-solving technique? Was justice done? Why wasn't there a discussion held to see who would put the money to best use?

BREAKING IN

Topic: The feelings of being left out and of being part of a group.
Purpose: To explore feelings, cliques, friendship. To help grow closer.
This is a technique borrowed from encounter groups. It works best with a small group of about seven or eight.

The group stands in a tight circle and locks arms. One person remains outside the circle. The person must try as hard as possible to get inside the circle; the group tries as hard as it can to keep that person out. The person can try to talk or climb his way in. When he does break in, he becomes part of the circle. Then another person takes his place outside and tries to break in. Each person takes a turn being outside the group.

The ability of this game to generate feelings is amazing. A person outside does indeed have a sense of isolation, of being left out. After a few unsuccessful attempts to break in, the outsider begins to feel somewhat desperate. The group begins to feel closer together, united in a common task, even if only keeping someone else out. A room with a fair amount of open space is needed for this exercise.

Afterward the group discusses the feelings during the game: how it felt to be out, how it felt to be keeping someone else out, how it felt to fail and succeed, what techniques were used by various participants.

BUT I WAS JUST FOLLOWING ORDERS

Topic: Conformity, crowd psychology.
Purpose: To see if the class or group is influenced by group action; to provide an experience that introduces topics such as conformity, crowd psychology, repression, freedom, following orders.

Would you have obeyed Hitler if assigned to Dachau?

What would you have done if you were at My Lai? "I certainly wouldn't have massacred people" goes the most common answer. But what if you were ordered to shoot anyone and everyone upon sight? How far would you go in following orders?

In the early 1960s, a Yale psychologist conducted some experiments in which volunteers were placed in a position where they thought they were giving shocks to innocent victims in an attempt to reinforce learning. The shocks were labeled in intensity from slight to 450 volts. In spite of the fact that at 190 volts the supposed victim screamed "I can't stand the pain," a significant percent of the volunteers went to 450 volts. Not one of the volunteers stopped short of administering what he believed to be a shock of 300 volts. Over 1,000 people were tested, and the overwhelming majority were very obedient in giving shocks to innocent recipients. (For a filmed account of this experiment, see the film *Obedience*, p. 82.)

Just how susceptible people are to following authority for its own sake or to following the crowd can be determined by a few do-it-yourself experiments.

All you have to do is get a small group in the class to do something for no apparent reason—like get up and leave the class in the middle of a sentence. See how many, if any, follow simply because that's what everyone else is doing.

Discuss the current hair or dress styles in regard to conformity. Keep discussion on the "I wear this style because . . ." level rather than the "I think they want . . ." level.

With some careful planning and a bit of construction a most interesting experiment can be set up based on the work of Dr. Richard Crutchfield. He had five subjects seated close to each other, but screened off so that no one could see others. Each booth had a panel of switches to signal answers of questions given to the group. The lights were signals indicating what answers the other four members gave to the questions. The subjects were told that their position would be identified by the letters *A, B, C, D,* and *E*. However, upon entering the booth each discovered that he was *E*.

The experimenter asked multiple-choice questions with a limited number of answers, such as, Which line is longer? The experimenter controlled the lights in the booths and made it appear that subjects *A, B, C,* and *D* all said *X* was longer. Yet *Y* was obviously the longer line.

Will the subject push the button indicating his belief even if it does go against what he believes the others answered? Dr. Crutchfield's experiments found that "given the right conditions almost everyone will desert the evidence of his senses or his own honest opinion and conform to the seeming consensus of the group." (Some high-level mathematicians even yielded to simple errors in arithmetic.)

It would be difficult, but not impossible, to work a similar experiment in a school. Some students know enough about wiring to rig up the simple light system, or clever ways could be found to do the experiment nonelectronically.

THE CIRCLE GAME

Topic: Feelings of trust, dependency; putting oneself in the hands of another.
Purpose: To help a group experience a growth in trust or its lack of mutual trust.

Groups of six to nine stand shoulder to shoulder in a circle. One person steps into the center of the circle, closes his eyes, and falls backward. He is caught and passed around the circle as gently as possible. The person in the center should keep his heels stationary and relaxed and allow the group to take over. Each person takes a turn in the center of the circle for about one minute; the group decides when each person can rejoin the circle. Any group member who lacks trust should receive a longer time in the center. This gives him the experience of what it feels like to receive support from the group. The group should adjust itself to accommodate the varying heights and weights of group members. The exercise should be carried out in silence; background music is often helpful.

After all the members have been in the center, they should discuss feelings. Were they tense? relaxed? Which people gave themselves to the experience? Which ones were rigid, afraid of falling?

CONFORM OR BE WRONG

Topic: Conformity.
Purpose: To see if a person will trust his senses or the incorrect views of others.

The teacher presents a number of perception problems for solution—for example, Which line is longer? Which figure is closest to a perfect circle? etc. One by one students are asked to say which figure is the correct answer to the teacher's questions.

The catch is that most of the students are in on the experiment while a few are not. Those who are in on the experiment all intentionally give the same wrong answer. The person who is not aware of the conspiracy is asked for his opinion last or near the end.

Dr. Richard Crutchfield found in a more elaborate experiment (see page 154) that "given the right conditions almost everyone will desert the evidence of his senses or his own honest opinion and conform to the seeming consensus of the group." He even found that some high-level mathematicians yielded to the false group consensus on some fairly easy arithmetic problems, giving wrong answers they would never have given under normal conditions.

The discussion could center on the topics of freedom and conformity. Care should be taken to avoid undue embarrassment to students.

Reference
Experiments conducted by Dr. Richard Crutchfield in 1955 as reported in Carl Rogers' *Freedom to Learn* (Columbus, Ohio: Merrill, 1969).

NON-SENSE WALK

Topic: Feelings of trust, dependency, the helping relationship.
Purpose: To help a group explore its need and ability to trust each other.

This is a technique often used in encounter groups. It is simple, non-threatening, and effective in eliciting feeling responses. It can be done with a group of any size.

Half the people in the group close their eyes, and the other half lead them on a walk around the room, building, or outdoors. A guide should not speak, using only a hand on the shoulder or arm to lead his partner. The person being led should try to keep his eyes closed throughout the entire walk. Blindfolds should definitely not be used.

After five to ten minutes a signal agreed upon previously should be given (necessarily one heard in the entire building), and each leader and "blind" person should exchange roles. Another signal indicates that the exercise is over and that the group should reassemble in the original location.

When everyone is reassembled, encourage participants to discuss their feelings while leading and being led. Very often guides run their partners into walls or other obstacles. Discuss if this was merely in fun or if there were other reasons. Have those who were misled tell their feelings.

Inquire if nearly everyone was unable to keep eyes closed for the entire blind period, and speculate on reasons for this. Does it reveal a lack of trust? A reflex response? The discussion might conclude by focusing on personal trust and risk-taking among group members.

It is often helpful to repeat the exercise after discussion to see if any change takes place. The goal should be movement that is as close to normal as possible. If partners feel confident in each other, they could try running or some other more complicated maneuvers.

WITH A LITTLE HELP FROM YOUR FRIENDS

Topic: Giving and receiving compliments.
Purpose: To help overcome the difficulty of giving and accepting praise; to strengthen positive group feelings; to provide a joyful and uplifting experience.

The ideal group size for this exercise is nine or ten although almost any size group can make it work if enough time is available. Many groups can operate simultaneously in the same room.

The group members sit in a circle and one person volunteers to be first. The others in the group give him honest compliments. The person receiving the compliments should not make any reply to the group. Each person in the group takes a turn receiving compliments from the others.

There should be no discussion when compliments are being given. But after the experience participants should talk about the feelings they had during the session, especially when receiving compliments. Discussion should later proceed to why people often become embarrassed or even defensive when they are praised. It is common to brush off praise with the equivalent of "It was nothing, really." Compare such responses to defense mechanisms.

This seemingly simple exercise usually creates a warm feeling among people and serves as a basis for growth within the group.

WORLD-CHAMPIONSHIP PAPER-AIRPLANE CONTEST

Topic: Group process, contribution of skills to a group task.
Purpose: To observe and discuss contributions of individuals to a group process.

Q: Why do most classrooms have high ceilings?
A: So that paper airplanes can fly better.

The fascination of paper airplanes extends from sixth-graders to scientists. The usually staid and scholarly *Scientific American* magazine ran a paper-plane contest a couple of years ago that drew nationwide entries from kids and physicists alike. I even entered my humble design. I received a letter from *Scientific American* saying that I didn't win but that it was creative efforts such as mine that produced the Michelangelos and Wright brothers. I felt good at least.

What could be more natural to a classroom than the experience of building a superb paper airplane? First, divide the group or class into two equal groups. One group acts as observers, and the other as participants. Then divide the participants and observers into separate groups of four or five persons each. Each group of observers should, if possible, sit in a circle outside the circle formed by the plane makers.

Once this is done, give out the instruction sheets. The plane makers should not be told what the observers' directions say. The contest should be carried out according to the rules outlined on the Participants' Instruction Sheet, and one group's design should be selected as the winner.

After fifteen minutes of building and the judging, observers and participants in each group should discuss how each of the builders took part in the group process. Each builder should reflect back on his behavior and see clearly how he operated and why.

The process should then be repeated with the roles reversed. The builders' behavior might be different because they know they are being observed. Discuss the differences between the two sessions and the reasons for them. Did the second session produce a better plane with less effort?

Participants' Instruction Sheet for Airplane Contest
Your group is to compete with the other groups to produce the world's
best paper airplane. You must use the paper provided but can add any
of your own material. Your group must produce *one* plane. Here is
how the final planes will be judged:

Airworthiness Ten points for every second the plane remains in
the air. Time is kept from the time the plane leaves your hand until it
makes contact with some other object. A plane that stays in the air for
3.2 seconds would receive 32 points.

Accuracy Planes will be thrown at a target from 12 feet. Each
plane will be thrown at the target twice and will receive 10 points for
each hit. The target could be a window or area of a wall or blackboard.

Design Ten points will be awarded by the judge to those planes
which show some attempt at artistic design.

You will have fifteen minutes. The judge will provide timings for
any plane presented before the fifteen-minute deadline. Timing should
be done with a stopwatch.

Observers' Instruction Sheet for Airplane Contest
You are to select one participant in the group to observe. You are to
watch him during the entire contest and notice how he contributes to
or keeps from the group his talents. Decide what role he plays in the
group's attempt to design and build the paper plane. The group's task
is to design and build a paper plane that will stay in the air the longest,
will fly most accurately, and will look best.

Here are some common roles that people play in groups:

1. The take-charge guy	He thinks he's the only one in the group with any ability.
2. The do-nothing	This person sits off to the side and makes no contribution to the group.
3. The dart thrower	This person throws darts at almost any idea suggested by anyone else but rarely, if ever, offers a better idea.
4. The soapbox	This person talks and talks and talks.
5. The clique	This is a part of the entire group that actually does the work. They make the others feel unwanted and do the work themselves.

6. The coordinator	This person takes charge but accepts the ideas of others. He does feel that others in the group can help.
7. The mediator	This person helps keep peace in the group. He acts as a go-between for people and thereby helps the smooth flow of ideas.
8. The follower	This is the yes man. He or she simply says yes whenever a strong person makes a suggestion.
9. The traveler	This person seems more interested in the activities of the other groups than in his own.

THE GOOD SAMARITAN EXPERIMENT

Topic: Apathy.
Purpose: To see and experience when people will go out of their way to help someone in need.

Are Good Samaritans the rule or the exception? Stories of people beaten while a crowd watches appear with sickening regularity in the papers, but so do stories of heroic rescues. When are people likely to give and receive help?

A now almost classic study conducted by John M. Darley of Princeton and Bibb Latane of Ohio State found that a bystander is less likely to become involved when he is part of a group than when he is alone. When part of a group, he takes the attitude that "someone else will help," and often the "someone else" never shows up. When a person is alone he feels a greater responsibility to help.

It's one thing to read reports of experiments and another to plan and execute a class experiment on the subject of apathy versus involvement. One class of high school students in Chicago had three volunteers (gleefully) fake a sidewalk beating of a fourth volunteer. They left him lying there to see what would happen. A student with a camera hid across the street and recorded the reactions of passersby. A similar experiment could be conducted without staging the fight. Usually someone in a class has access to a super 8 camera, and everyone can contribute to purchase film.

Such an experiment could be part of a larger study of the question of detachment and alienation. One of the best treatments of this topic is an article by Nat Hentoff, "The Cold Society," which appeared in the September 1966 issue of *Playboy*.

Darley and Latane's study can be found in the December 1968 *Psychology Today* or can be purchased for $.50 (plus $.05 postage and handling; minimum handling charge is $.25) from Psychology Today Reader Service, Box 4788, Clinton, Iowa 52732.

LOST LETTERS

Topic: Prejudice.
Purpose: To expand the concept of prejudice beyond the racial connotation it now has; to measure the effect and presence of prejudice in the "man in the street."

Volunteers should address envelopes (the more envelopes, the more valid the results) to fictitious organizations. Half should be addressed to groups with patriotic or highly "positive" names, such as Committee for Crime Prevention, Highway Safety Society. The other half should be addressed to groups such as the Organization for Socialism, Communist Teaching Society, the Radical's Journal.

Address all the envelopes to the same place and make arrangements for their delivery. A postal box might be rented for a quarter year for under ten dollars, or a willing parent could help by providing a home or business address or box. If nothing can be arranged, make sure there is a valid return address, and use a fictitious address.

Paper or an ambiguous letter should be placed inside the envelope, so it is not obviously empty. Students should then "lose" each sealed and stamped envelope on some city sidewalk. They should keep tallies for the next two weeks on the percentage of each type of envelope returned.

Try to predict the results. Will people tend to mail any letter, or are they selective? Are people's good deeds influenced by their political beliefs? What do the results show?

Reference
"The Lost Letter Technique," *Psychology Today,* June 1969.

MONOPOLY

Topic: Attitudes toward poverty.
Purpose: To concretize economic discrimination against minorities.
Have enough Monopoly games so that the entire group can play the game. Before beginning each group should draw up a new set of rules, in which half the players belong to a dark-skinned minority group and half are whites. The rules should favor the whites and impair the others' chance of winning. This experiment might be used in conjunction with a study of the existing conditions in the city or might introduce such a research project.

In devising the game, students can compose different sets of Chance and Community Chest cards, establish different fees that the players receive when passing Go, decide on different criteria for going to and getting out of jail, and zone certain neighborhoods "For Whites Only." Rules should be based on existing conditions insofar as possible. Students should be given the opportunity to play the game from both sides, and feelings should be discussed when the game is finished.

An example of a professional attempt at a project similar to this is *The Cities Game* by Psychology Today Games. *The Cities Game* is designed to provide an experience of negotiating and political bargaining.

RED, WHITE, AND BLUE VALUES

Topic: American values, respect for freedom, rights of the individual.
*Purpose: To determine if Americans recognize and value the freedoms
and rights set down in our historical documents.*
Around July Fourth each year, a number of groups conduct an experiment which seems to have uniformly consistent results, no matter where tried.

Show some people a copy of the Bill of Rights, the Declaration of Independence, or the First Amendment, and without identifying the document, ask people if they agree with the sentiments expressed.

Note reactions, compile results, and discuss implications. The experience students gain by actually approaching people about basic values is often more valuable than the results of the experiment itself.

At a West German military base, 252 U.S. soldiers heard the Declaration of Independence and were asked to sign the statement if they agreed, not to sign if they didn't. Seventy-three percent refused to sign. When the same approach was used with civilians in Miami, only one person out of 50 agreed to sign. A number called the statement "Commie junk," and threatened to call the police.

A Massachusetts high school group circulated the First Amendment (freedom of religion, speech, press, assembly, and petition) among 1,154 people. 4 percent recognized the First Amendment; 42 percent agreed with it; 35 percent disagreed, and 23 percent refused to commit themselves.

TELEVIOLENCE

Topic: Violence on television.
Purpose: To increase awareness of the amount of violence on television and to discuss its implications and effects.

In our culture, nudity in entertainment is a national scandal while violence is acceptable, even for kids. Attitudes toward explicit sex and violence in films reveals a social psychosis.

As recently as 1969 a film theater operator in Chicago was arrested and jailed for showing a B-grade skin flick that had already played in the city on seven other occasions. The owner was careful to restrict the audience for *Acapulco Uncensored* to adults. Meanwhile, back at numerous neighborhood theaters the grade-school crowd was lining up for kiddy matinees featuring a horror film—*Night of the Living Dead.* The film involves, among other delectables, a scene in which ghouls set fire to a pickup truck. When the teen-age couple inside is sufficiently barbecued, the ghouls rip apart their bodies and eat them. Many of the children in the audience found the scene genuinely horrifying, even to the point of tears. But the film passed by the Police Censor Board as acceptable for general viewing. As one local film critic observed, "The board passed the movie, I guess, because it had no nudity in it. Only cannibalism. Cannibalism is OK if you do it with your clothes on."

Films seem to be more violent than ever, but butchery on television has become at least slightly controversial since the assassinations. Only a week before Robert Kennedy was killed, a study of violence on television found that in eight hours the three networks and six local outlets showed "ninety-three specific incidents involving sadistic brutality, murder, cold-blooded killing, sexual cruelty and related sadism."

One Senate subcommittee heard evidence that "normal persons who see a violent film subsequently exhibit nearly twice as much violence as persons who have not seen such a film."

In the light of such studies and investigations, the networks agreed to lessen the amount of violence on the tube. How much violence remains and how necessary it is to the story can be the subject of a class research experiment. Assign students the task of watching for violence on television and logging violent acts on the chart that follows. Compare children's programs (Saturday morning) to adult fare; compare the three networks and the independent stations. Discuss the implications of the violence, whether it is a healthy release for violent tendencies in man or a vicious circle feeding the flames of violence. Compare results on the chart, and discuss why the violence was used in the shows and what effects it might have on the viewers. Look for patterns in the violence which indicate social values—e.g., self-defense, violence in the name of the law, violence against whomever is obviously a "bad guy."

Further reading

Violence and the Mass Media by Otto Larsen (New York: Harper & Row, 1969, paperback).

To Establish Justice, To Insure Domestic Tranquility: the Final Report of the National Commission on the Causes and Prevention of Violence (New York: Bantam Books, 1970, paperback), chapter 8, "Violence in Television Entertainment Programs."

Violence: America in the Sixties by Arthur Schlesinger, Jr. (New York: New American Library, 1968), chapter 4, "Televiolence."

YOU DON'T NEED A POSTMAN TO KNOW WHICH WAY THE MAIL FLOWS

Topic: Responsiveness of local or national government to criticism.
Purpose: To test the reactions of various government officials to criticism and praise.

This experiment was first conducted by a graduate student at Rutgers University. He wrote President Nixon five letters criticizing his Vietnam policy and received no answer. A sixth letter praised the president and offered support for his war policy. The sixth letter produced a

Times in 15 Min. Segments	Name of Program	N.W. or Ch.	Weapon	Injury Given	Inflicted by	Inflicted upon	Motive for Violence

response—a thanks for your "thoughtful concern for our country," complete with presidential seal and replica of Mr. Nixon's signature.

The experiment was conducted on only a very limited scale and was directed to only one public official. The results could be a mere coincidence. A class could easily try this experiment on a much larger scale and select other local and national government offices toward which to direct both its praise and criticism. Discussion should deal with a prediction of results and their implications.

MENTAL SET THEORY

Topic: Consciousness, formation of opinions.
Purpose: To determine if opinions are freely chosen or if they come in groups; to identify sets of beliefs that are often found together.

In *The Greening of America* Charles Reich notes: "Ask a stranger on a bus or airplane about psychiatry or redwoods or police or taxes or morals or war, and you can guess with fair accuracy his views on all the rest of these topics and many others besides, even though they are seemingly unrelated. If he thinks wilderness areas should be 'developed' he is quite likely to favor punitive treatment for campus disruptions. If he is enthusiastic about hunting animals, he probably believes that the American economic system rests on individual business activity, and has an aversion to people with long hair."

True? False? Exaggerated? Are opinions and beliefs related? Construct a theory on how beliefs are related, and test that theory through a survey of parents, students, or volunteers.

The *Los Angeles Free Press,* an underground newspaper, formulated a similar questionnaire. They asked four opinion questions concerning sex education being communist inspired, the right of government to tap telephones of the unpatriotic, the bombing of Red China, and abortion as a form of murder. The second part of the survey asked a logic question (A is larger than B; B is larger than C; therefore, C is larger than A) which had three possible answers—true, false, or maybe. The third part of the survey asked nine information questions related to the four opinion questions—Where is China? Who is their leader? What is a fetus? etc. The questionnaire results showed that those who were favorable to the four opinions given were those who were most likely to stumble on the logic questions and also those who answered the information questions incorrectly.

WHEN MASCULINITY AND FEMININITY ENSLAVE

Topic: Sexism.
Purpose: To prevent sex stereotypes from interfering with personal relations.

Sexism here means an attitude which leads one to limit the humanity of others according to sexual classification and narrow definitions of male and female. Like any form of prejudice, the attitude is both individual and structured into society, with both aspects feeding each other. This series of activities aims to increase awareness of the pervasiveness of sexism and to help effect a personal attitude change and lessen resistance to social change.

Detecting Sexism in the Group

Distribute a questionnaire with about four or five different items to be evaluated. Each item is a very brief description of a person, from which the person filling out the questionnaire is expected to draw tentative conclusions. The questionnaire is presented as a test in evaluating people on the basis of incomplete information. No mention should be made of sexism.

Half the group (or half of the groups) receives the questionnaire, while the other half is given a questionnaire identical in all respects, except that the names are changed from one sex to the other. While half the class is evaluating a candy company executive named John, the other half is judging the same executive, this time named Joan. The existence of two questionnaires should not be revealed before they are completed. The questionnaires are then evaluated by comparing the total of the responses of those who had the male names to those who had female names. Discussion follows the tabulation.

Here is one sample questionnaire. Remember to prepare a second version with each name changed to indicate the opposite sex.

Evaluations Based on Incomplete Information

From the limited information given about each person below, you are to make an educated guess as to some of that person's character traits.

Encircle one number on the rating scale; there are no right and wrong answers in this test.

1. John works at Bell Telephone Company, is married and has two children. He wears colorful clothes. He probably is:

INTELLIGENT	1	2	3	4	5	STUPID
COMPETENT	1	2	3	4	5	INCOMPETENT
RATIONAL	1	2	3	4	5	EMOTIONAL

2. Ruth is 18 years old and a sophomore college student. She is five feet, eight inches tall and has blond hair. She makes average grades and dates about once a week. She probably is:

ARTISTIC	1	2	3	4	5	SCIENTIFIC
AGGRESSIVE	1	2	3	4	5	PASSIVE
INDEPENDENT	1	2	3	4	5	DEPENDENT

3. James Day is 46 years old, a professional writer, is married and has three children. His wife also works, and they own their own home. He probably is:

SELF-CENTERED	1	2	3	4	5	OTHER-CENTERED
ATTRACTIVE	1	2	3	4	5	UNATTRACTIVE
CONTENT	1	2	3	4	5	AMBITIOUS

The questionnaire can be left with only three items to mark or could be expanded to six by composing three more descriptions but using the same eighteen descriptive adjectives.

Another approach to revealing sexist attitudes in a group is simply to ask group members to rate statements on a 1 to 5 scale with 1 representing total disagreement and 5, total agreement. This approach works well with groups that have not given much thought to the question of sex roles, woman's liberation, etc. With groups that already have strong opinions, this approach is either unnecessary or productive of more heat than light. Some statements which could be rated on a 1 to 5 basis are:

Men are less emotional than women.

The desire to give birth is natural to women.

Women are superior to men.

Men should be more tender and soft.

Women should run the household.

Fighting is natural to a man.

Women tend to be more artistic than men.

Men who have sexual experience before marriage most often make better husbands.

Women who have sexual experience before marriage most often make better wives.

A further variation on this idea involves using the value visualization technique described on page 42. Read the above statements and others to the class, and have them physically position themselves, with one side of the room representing agreement and the other, disagreement. Have people explain why they move from one position to another.

A more extensive Test for Sexism can be conducted if a large group —a school or organization—can participate. A controversial one-page essay should be duplicated; the subject matter is not important. Half the copies should be identified as written by a male author, the other half by a female author (say, John Rivers and Joan Rivers). To make sure participants are aware of the author, the essay should begin with a paragraph about the author, giving biographical information and identifying the author as highly competent. The biography should be identical on both versions of the essay with only the name changed.

Half the people in each group tested should receive the essay identified as written by a female, and the other half, the same essay identified as written by a male. Participants should be prevented from looking at others' papers, as in a test. If this should prove too difficult, simply give every other group tested the different versions.

The group tested should believe that your main concern is with the views expressed in the essay. Ask them to rate the essay and provide 1 to 5 scales at the end based on writing style, force of argument, cogency of main point, etc. Each reader should rate the essay on these points.

Results should be compared to see if the female papers receive consistently lower ratings than the male papers.

Detecting Sexism in Media and Advertising

Observe television, both programming and commercials, for one week, paying close attention to the use of male and female stereotypes. At the end of one week, compare the results, discuss the implications, perhaps even take some positive action by contacting TV stations and the national networks. Note especially elements of stereotype.

Time	Net-work	Program or Product Advertised	Character of Female	Character of Male

Advertising Simply gather a collection of sexist ads, and display and discuss them. Also compare both advertising and editorial content of men's and women's magazines.

Quotes for Thought and Discussion

Woman

Women are essential to the economy not only as free labor, but also as consumers. The American system of capitalism depends for its survival on the consumption of vast amounts of socially wasteful goods, and a prime target for the unloading of this waste is the housewife. She is the purchasing agent for the family. . . . Although she spends the wealth, she does not own or control it—it simply passes through her hands (Marlene Dixon, "Why Women's Liberation?" in *Ramparts*).

The closest I've been able to come to what's wrong is that men have a greater sense of self than women have. Marriage is an aspect of men's lives, whereas it is the very center of most women's lives, the whole of their lives. It seemed to me that women felt they couldn't exist except in the eyes of men—that if a man wasn't looking at them or attending to them, then they just weren't there (Lucy Komisar, "The New Feminism," *Saturday Review*, 21 February 1970).

Feelings, moods and attitudes . . . rule a woman, not facts, reason or logic. . . . The acquisition of knowledge or responsibilities does not lessen women's need for support, guidance and control. Quite the contrary (G. C. Payetter, *How to Get and Hold a Woman*).

As blacks were defined and limited socially by their color, so women are defined and limited by their sex. . . . The very stereotypes that express the society's belief in the biological inferiority of women recall the images used to justify the oppression of blacks. The nature of women, like that of slaves, is depicted as dependent, incapable of reasoned thought, childlike in its simplicity and warmth, martyred in the role of mother, and mystical in the role of sexual partner (Marlene Dixon in *Ramparts*).

Mothers will have to stop grooming daughters from childhood on for marriage and motherhood. Men will have to accept and work with women as full partners in decision-making in all areas that affect human society. Advertisers will have to stop selling products by showing women only as teenage playgirls whose sole purpose is housekeeping. And women themselves will have to forego the luxury of dependence by assuming the burdens of a separate and equal identity (Marya Mannes).

Man

The all-sensory, all-pervasive total environment of the future may be no place for the narrow-gauge, specialized male. Emotional range and psychic mobility may be valued. Heightened intuition may be required. The breed of hombre generally portrayed by John Wayne is already an anachronism. "Be a man!" the hombre bellows, and the more perceptive of our young laugh (George B. Leonard, *The Man & Woman Thing.* [New York: Dell, 1971]).

The male almost invariably attaches inordinate importance to position, to his own if he enjoys a distinguished or superior one, and to the position of others if his own is lowly. He wants to have it known where he stands in relation to other men, and his standing must be confirmed by means of titles, slots, washroom keys, parking space assignments, classifications, and possessions. . . . With men an assurance of status has been long essential; with women it is likely to be imitative and a pastime (Charles W. Ferguson, *The Male Attitude* [Boston: Little, Brown, 1966]).

The traditional image of the American male, strong, hardheaded, decisive, does not apply to the majority of contemporary men. The description might better be applied to American culture generally, since that often appears rather rigid, compulsive, and aggressive. . . . In a highly organized society whose economy is dominated by the great, bureaucratically structured corporations and whose education so often resembles a kind of industrial processing, it is difficult for the male to take genuine initiative in the conduct of his life (Hendrik Ruitenbeek, *The Male Myth* [New York: Dell, 1967]).

A modern Hindu sage has remarked that the first thing he has to teach Westerners who come to him is how to cry, which also goes to show that our spontaneity is inhibited not only by the ego-complex as such but also by the Anglo-Saxon conception of masculinity. So far from being a form of strength, the masculine rigidity and toughness which we affect is nothing more than an emotional paralysis. It is assumed not because we are in control of our feelings but because we fear them along with everything in our nature that is symbolically feminine and yielding. But a man who is emotionally paralyzed cannot be male, that is, he cannot be male in relation to female, for if he is to relate himself to a woman there must be something of the woman in his nature (Alan Watts, *Nature: Man and Woman* [New York: Random House, 1970]).

It might be in order to revise our ideas about what the proper sex role is for our boys and girls, and how best to train for it. Society needs men who are not limited to the so-called tougher masculine characteristics. An acquaintance of mine from India put it more simply: "the trouble with American men is they have no normal outlets for their femininity" (Faubion Bowers, "The Sexes: Getting It All Together," *Saturday Review,* 9 January 1971).

Short Films
It is perhaps a result of sexism that there are few really good short films about sexual stereotypes, if any.

Radcliffe Blues
A woman speaks on women's rights, alienation, and radicalization.
Directed by Claudia Weil.
(23 min., b&w, sale $175, rental $35, special rates to high schools)
Unfolding
An aesthetic expression of human sexuality from a woman's point of
view. Directed by Constance Beeson.
(18 min., b&w, sale $200, rental $40)
(Both from American Documentary Films, Inc., 336 West 84th Street,
New York, N.Y. 10024, or 379 Bay Street, San Francisco, Calif. 94133.)

Modern Women: The Uneasy Life
An NET documentary that explores the feelings of college-educated
women about the roles available to them in society. There are interviews with those living the traditional role of mother and housewife
as well as with those who have chosen careers. Not a Women's Lib
film.
(16 min., b&w, sale $200, rental $12, order #CS-1750; Indiana University, Audio-Visual Center, Bloomington, Ind. 47401.)

Up Against the Wall Miss America
A newsreel on the disruption of the 1969 Miss America pageant.
(7 min., rental $10; Newsreel, 28 West 31st Street, New York, N.Y.
10001; Newsreel probably has more recent releases on the woman's
liberation movement.)

Portrait of a Girl
The artificiality of our concept of feminine beauty, shown by a girl
applying makeup to her face. The film has won awards and could
accurately be subtitled: An extreme close-up and meditation on a
girl applying makeup.
(4 min., b&w, $6 rental; Center Cinema Co-op, c/o Columbia College,
540 N. Lake Shore Drive, Chicago, Illinois 60611.)

The American Woman in the 20th Century
A Metromedia TV documentary from before the days of radical
feminism. A documentary cavalcade of the American woman from
Gibson Girl to suffragette to flapper to Rosie the Riveter to Marilyn

Monroe. The final image of woman presented is as "emerging from the shelter of the Victorian era to become the captive Goddess of today's split-level suburbia."
(50 min., b&w, $250 sale, $25 rental; 19 min., $119 sale, rental $12, FI.)

Masculinity and Femininity
(Two 87-frame filmstrips with recorded narration)
Part I illustrates traditional labeling of occupations, sexual standards, personality traits, physical manner, and other factors as masculine or feminine. Students hear a young couple describe an experiment in switching roles. The program explores psychological reasons behind the aggressive-male and passive-female stereotypes. Part II includes a discussion by Margaret Mead and Marshall McLuhan on the possible effects of continuing role modification. Unisex fashions are reviewed as is the role of the sexes in other cultures.
($40 with LP's, $44 on cassettes; Guidance Associates, Pleasantville, N.Y. 10570.)

On Being a Woman and the New Feminists
A series of taped talks and discussions. Catalog and descriptions of each tape free.
(Pacifica Tape Library, 2217 Shattuck Ave., Berkeley, Calif. 94704.)

RELATIVITY PARABLES

Topic: The concept of the relativity of ideas.
Purpose: To help students examine their own ideas of what is subjective and objective and of what is definitive and what is relative.

In a very real sense we can never see things as *they are,* contrary to the popular expression which seems to indicate that we can. Instead, we see things as *we* are. Everything we see is filtered through our "censory" system; seeing is as much a psychological process as a biological one. Therefore, there is no such thing as total objectivity, only varying degrees of subjectivity.

To help in dealing with the concepts of relativity (outside of a physics class) and subjectivity, tell the class the following "parables," and examine the responses they generate.

The World Doubled Last Night
Tell the students that last night while they were all asleep the entire
universe doubled in size. Try to have them prove that it did not. Of
course, all the scales and rulers also doubled in size, so measuring will
be no good. The real question is that if everything changes in the same
degree and in the same relation as everything else, is there really any
change at all?

Man and the Train
A man was born on a train. This train is constantly moving at a single
speed, encircling the globe without stopping. The man born on the
train has never been outside the train. His only knowledge comes from
what he can see outside the windows. He is now sixteen years old; he
has never read about the outside world or been told by anyone what it
is like. The question is, what is his view of the world and what would
happen if the train would stop?

His world view would be that the world is moving steadily in a
single direction and that it is shaped like a strip. He would consider
himself stationary and the world moving, and not the other way around.
When the train would stop, the shock would be the same as that experienced by us if the world stopped moving very noticeably one day.
The train's stopping would shatter his world view and would perhaps
remain forever incomprehensible to him.

The Tale of the Adventurous Ant
One day an ant was assigned his first tasks outside the anthill. He was
told to drag back a dead grasshopper killed by the elders in a raid the
previous day.

Out he went, our young hero. Upon exiting from the anthill, he
was profoundly impressed and even shocked at the size of the outside
world. He had heard tales that the world was larger than his own world,
but never had he experienced such massive size.

At once he scurried in search of the grasshopper. As he continued
his search, carefully following detailed directions, he came to a barrier
that he could not surmount. So he did what any good ant would do;
he crawled under.

Upon so doing, he was again confronted with a shock that would
have caused a heart attack in any weaker ant. The world was immense-
ly larger than he had dreamed. For it seemed that the anthill had been

located under a bushel basket and what he had thought was the outside world was only the area covered by the basket. But now he was faced with the whole world. He realized that he really had been unable to understand his environment until he had gotten out of it. Only now did he see that the anthill was covered by a bushel basket.

He still had not found his grasshopper, so he continued on. Again a barrier stopped him until he was able to burrow under it. And another shock greeted him. For once on the other side of the barrier he realized that the bushel basket was located in a greenhouse and that what he had thought was the big wide world was really only a small greenhouse. Now that he was outside the greenhouse he could understand.

Well, the story goes on because it turns out that the ant, intelligent as he might be, still didn't know where he was. For the greenhouse was located just outside center field of the Astrodome in Houston. And, you see, that ant really isn't any different from you or me.

Blind Justice

There was once a man with one eye. He was considered handicapped and so was seldom given anything of importance to do in the world. He longed for power, like most men, and blamed his half sight for his lack of power.

One day he was whisked away to a land where everyone was blind. He quickly felt a great sense of power at his sudden superiority to everyone. He decided that he would serve these people and tell them the wonders of sight. He began to do so and expected a royal reception. Instead he found himself locked up and considered insane. There might be many people like the one-eyed man in the land of the blind among us today.

The Man Born Blind

This little story is based on a seventeenth-century letter by Molyneux to John Locke.

Once there was a man born blind who had been taught to distinguish by touch between a cube and a sphere of the same material. One day he was cured of his blindness. Shortly thereafter a cube and sphere of the same metal were placed in front of him. Would he, using his sense of sight, be able to tell which was the sphere and which was the cube?

CHECKING OUT THE SCHOOL—A SERIES OF ACTIVITIES

Topic: Student's own education.
Purpose: To encourage students to think about their own schooling, to involve students more in school, and to raise questions which any self-renewing school should ask itself.

One of the most interesting sections of most of my classes in the past years has been that in which we examined the school and American education with a critical eye. The purpose of the unit was to enable the students who stayed in the system to remain relatively safe from its adverse effects and to understand the system of which they were a part. Such a unit might begin merely as a gripe session, but should progress far deeper. Some of the more effective learning experiences that were included in these units were:

Hectograph and discuss a selection of quotes from people such as A. S. Neill, John Holt, George Leonard, Postman and Weingartner, Paul Goodman, and Edgar Friedenberg.

Send out a small group of students (or the entire class if the school is large or the class small) with the instructions that they are simply to walk around the school for fifteen minutes and return to the classroom. They are to view the school as if they were from another planet and know nothing about the purpose of the building. Upon returning, they should report what they saw and what happened to them.

Have the class draw up a Bill of Rights for High School Students. The Bill of Rights could include items on dress codes, lockers, records, punishment, grades, regulations, suspension and expulsion, tracking, and required attendance. Research the area of the constitutional rights of teen-agers.

Have the class design the school they would like to attend. This could be done as either a utopian scheme, with little regard to practicality, or it could be done with a view toward presenting the plan as a viable alternative for their next year.

Find out what records are kept on each student, who has access to them, how they are compiled, and the reason for their existence. Find out if students can see their own files. If not, why not?

If the school offers elective courses suggest that the student council or school paper publish an impartial student evaluation of the courses and teachers so that students could make choices with more information.

Suggest that teachers be evaluated by the students each year. Make a practical proposal on how this could be done.

Examine the role of student government in the schools. Is it a puppet government with carefully controlled membership (controlled usually before election), or does it have any real responsibility beyond dances and the dirty work connected with various school activities?

Study various methods used to evaluate student work, and propose a better one than that currently used. Try to establish the real basis for failing grades, and seek any consistent patterns in grading.

Ask and answer the 138 questions about the school suggested on pages 44-49 of *The Soft Revolution* by Neil Postman and Charles Weingartner (New York: Delta, 1971).

Study textbooks used in the school for biases, racist and sexist attitudes, propaganda, accuracy, and outdated concepts.

Examine the role of the clock in school.

Discuss ways to make the school more democratic, and implement at least one of the suggestions.

PPENDIX I

FILM SOURCES
Films can be rented by mail for a single showing for from $5 to $50.
University film libraries have prices 20 to 50% lower than the commercial distributors but are also more likely to have films booked months in advance and have prints in poor condition. Free catalogs are available from the commercial distributors listed below. University libraries frequently charge a one- to three-dollar fee for a large catalog.

AB	Audio/Brandon
	34 Macquesten Pkwy. South
	Mount Vernon, N.Y. 10550

ACI	ACI Films, Inc.
	35 West 45th St.
	New York, N.Y. 10036

AIM	Association Instructional Materials
	600 Madison Ave.
	New York, N.Y. 10022
	(plus eight regional offices)

AUGS	Augsburg Films
	426 South 5th St.
	Minneapolis, Minn. 55415

BFA

Bailey Film Associates
2211 Michigan Ave.
Santa Monica, Calif. 90404

BYU

Brigham Young University
Educational Media Services
Provo, Utah 84601

CCC

Canyon Cinema Co-op
Room 220, Industrial Center Bldg.
Sausalito, Calif. 94965

CCM

CCM Films, Inc.
866 Third Ave.
New York, N.Y. 10022

CAROUSEL

Carousel Films
1501 Broadway
New York, N.Y. 10036

CF

Contemporary Films/McGraw-Hill, Inc.
Princeton Rd.
Hightstown, N.J. 08520

828 Custer Ave.
Evanston, Ill. 60202

1714 Stockton St.
San Francisco, Calif. 94133

CFS

Creative Film Society
14558 Valerio St.
Van Nuys, Calif. 91405

CHURCHILL

Churchill Films
662 N. Robertson Blvd.
Los Angeles, Calif. 90069

CU

University of Colorado
Bureau of Audiovisual Instruction
Boulder, Colo. 80302

EBF

Encyclopedia Britannica Films
425 N. Michigan Ave.
Chicago, Ill. 60611
(and regional offices)

FDI

Film Distributors International
2221 South Olive St.
Los Angeles, Calif. 90007

FI

Films Incorporated
1144 Wilmette Ave.
Wilmette, Ill. 90091

FSU

Florida State University
Educational Media Center
Tallahassee, Fla. 32306

HARTLEY

Hartley Productions
279 East 44th St.
New York, N.Y. 10017

KING

King Screen Productions
320 Aurora Ave. North
Seattle, Wash. 98109

KSU

Audio-Visual Services
Kent State University
Kent, Ohio 44240

LCA

Learning Corporation of America
711 Fifth Ave.
New York, N.Y. 10022

MGH	McGraw-Hill Films 327 West 41st St. New York, N.Y. 10036 (and regional offices)
MMM	Mass Media Ministries 2116 N. Charles St. Baltimore, Md. 21218
MSU	Michigan State University Instructional Media Center East Lansing, Mich. 48823
NAVC	National Audio-Visual Center General Services Administration Washington, D.C. 20409
NBC	National Broadcasting Co. Educational Enterprises, Room 1040 30 Rockefeller Plaza New York, N.Y. 10020
NU	University of Nevada Audiovisual Communication Center Reno, Nev. 89507
NYU	New York University Film Library 26 Washington Pl. New York, N.Y. 10003
PE	Perennial Education 1825 Willow Rd. Northfield, Ill. 60093
PSU	Pennsylvania State University Audio-Visual Services University Park, Pa. 16802

PYRAMID

Pyramid Films
Box 1048
Santa Monica, Calif. 90406

ROA

Roa's Films
1696 N. Astor St.
Milwaukee, Wis. 53202

SUNYB

State University of N.Y. at Buffalo
Instructional Communications Center
Media Library
22 Foster Annex
Buffalo, N.Y. 14214

TIME-LIFE

Time-Life Films
43 West 16th St.
New York, N.Y. 10011

UC

Extension Media Center
University of California
Berkeley, Calif. 94720

UIll

Visual Aids Service
University of Illinois
Division of University Extension
704 South Sixth St.
Champaign, Ill. 61820

UInd

Audio-Visual Center
University of Indiana
Bloomington, Ind. 47401

UM

University of Michigan
Audio-Visual Education Center
416 Fourth St.
Ann Arbor, Mich. 48103

UMn

Department of Audio Visual Extension
General Extension Division
University of Minnesota
2037 University Ave., S.E.
Minneapolis, Minn. 55455

USC

University of Southern California
Film Distribution Section
University Pl.
Los Angeles, Calif. 90007

USF

University of Southern Florida
Film Service
Tampa, Fla. 33626

UU

University of Utah
Extension Media Center
Milton Bennion Hall 207
Salt Lake City, Utah 84110

WU

University of Wyoming
Audiovisual Services
Attn: Booking Clerk
Laramie, Wyo. 82070

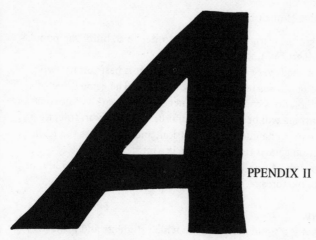

PPENDIX II

SIMULATION GAMES AVAILABLE FOR PURCHASE

Baldicer
Baldicer is a simulation game dealing with food production and distribution. It is designed to stimulate interest in a study of the complex problems of feeding the world's population in an age in which the skill is available, but has remained unused. The game gives its 10-20 players an experience of the interdependence involved in feeding the world.

Each player is a food coordinator responsible for the survival of 150 million people. In order to keep the people alive, a player must have at least one Baldicer (Balanced Diet Certificate) at all times. If a player loses all his Baldicers, his people are dead, and he becomes part of the world conscience, whose job it is to urge other food coordinators to cooperate to keep people alive.

Baldicers are earned by work performed in a 40-second work period. The work consists of writing the words *dig, sweat, push, pull* on a magic slate as often as possible. Baldicers are gained for work and are changed in value by food machines, inflation, population growth, and natural forces. Each player keeps his own score on a large tally sheet at times reminiscent of the Income Tax Form 1040.

The catch of the game is that all but two players begin the game with 5 Baldicers; the other two have 35 and 50 respectively. This is intended to roughly represent a world in which 20 percent of the world's population has 50 percent of the wealth. In the course of playing the game, some groups learn to cooperate in order to stabilize the population, while others fail to achieve this.

The game needs very careful preparation. It is best run by two people, although this is not absolutely essential. The game director's instruction book does contain all the needed information, but some extra page turning will be needed to find it. The ability to tolerate a noisy classroom, to handle mass confusion, and to process the feelings and information gained from the game is a must.

$25 from John Knox Press, Box 1176, Richmond, Va. 23209, or from some bookstores.

Confrontation

Confrontation is a simulation game in which students and protesters interact with various establishment teams to try to change the system. Establishment groups include the university administration, business, military, city hall, financial community, Washington, state government, landlords, and homeowners. The game is basically a role-playing simulation for 4-20 players which allows participants to express and react to viewpoints they might otherwise only read about in newspapers.

$6 from John N. Hansen Co., Western Merchandise Mart, 1355 Market St., San Francisco, Calif. 94103.

Dignity

Dignity is a human relations game that produces in its players the same sort of frustration experienced by black ghetto dwellers. It is a twisted sort of ghetto Monopoly where instead of collecting $200 for passing Go, players are more likely to move back five spaces because "your baby daughter just ate some paint that fell off the wall into her bed."

The object of the board game is to move to the game's goal, labeled "dignity," debt free. Play money, dice, and instruction cards are used.

Players find themselves making statements such as "I didn't want to move forward; I'd be better off going backwards." They then realize, if sensitive to the purpose of the game, that this is exactly the same feeling many ghetto blacks live with. It is also the same feeling which prompts action that white middle-class America can comprehend only as laziness. To a small degree, the players crawl into the ill-fitting skin of the inner city and find it devastating.

The game can be played by 2-4 people and is available from Friendship Press, 475 Riverside Dr., New York, N.Y. 10027, for $4.95.

Empire

Empire demonstrates the place of American colonists in the British Empire and explains how their membership in the empire affected the way they made their living. *Empire* was designed for the junior high and high school level and takes three to five hours to play.

Players are divided into seven teams, which include British West Indies planters, London merchants, and colonial farmers. Each team starts the game with goods to sell and consumer demands to be met. In each play, participants bargain for prices, buy and sell merchandise, and move their ships across the Atlantic.

During the game players encounter a London monopoly, arbitrary trade laws, the risks of smuggling and piracy, the Royal Navy as protector or law enforcer, and other aspects of the colonial empire.

Available from KDI Instructional Systems, 1810 MacKenzie, Columbus, Ohio 43220.

Extinction

One of the best of the many board games designed to teach about ecology is Sinaeur Associates' *Extinction*. The game is playable by 2-4 students at a time (up to 8 if partners are used), and can be taught in fifteen minutes by a teacher who is familiar with the game. It is inexpensive (about $11.95) and involves enough strategy and decision-making to hold interest of students from upper elementary level to adult.

The game includes a board on which the Island of Darwinia is pictured and used as a playing surface and 80 dice, 210 direction cards, and a fine 16-page explanation booklet. The object of the game is simply to survive, while eliminating the other players.

The game can be played a number of times as an inductive learning experience followed by discussion or it can be used to demonstrate technical terms, such as *population density, dispersion, quantified population dispersion, natality and mortality, predator-prey interaction, two-species competition,* and *mutualism.* Extinction is more than a simple game which teaches population vocabulary; it can also be used for rather technical demonstrations of population control dynamics. Extinction is by far the most versatile of the ecology games yet to appear.

Each player populates the island and is given seven allies which constitute his genotype. By preying on vulnerable species, moving into areas most conducive to growth and reproducing, each player attempts to solidify his own position. The first time, or even the first two times, through the game without much introduction, the students will not see the strategy that enables them to survive, but gradually will figure out winning strategies and thus learn about special survival.

$11.95 from Sinaeur Associates, Inc., 20 Second St., Stanford, Conn. 06905.

Generation Gap

Generation Gap simulates the interaction between a parent and adolescent son or daughter. In this game either real parents and teens or role-playing adults and teens interact and compete with their counterparts at other boards in the room. The parent's score is determined by the teen's behavior (which he indicates on the board) and the teen's score jointly by his own behavior and by parental punishment, if any. Each round of the game starts with a few minutes of discussion between parent and teen-ager, during which they may try to reach agreement on how the teen will behave. On any issue where agreement is not reached, the parent gives an order to the teen-ager. The teen then selects his behavior; he may violate agreements and/or disobey orders. The parent can, within certain constraints, punish the teen (subtract points) if disobedience or violation of agreement occurs.

The game is suited for almost any age grouping from early adolescent to adult. Accommodates 4 to 10 players and takes 30 to 60 minutes. Costs $15 from Western Publishing Co., School and Library Dept., 850 Third Ave., New York, N.Y. 10022.

Ghetto

Ghetto bridges the gap between intellectual study of poverty and desperation and actual firsthand experience. With the use of easy to follow role guides and a simplified model of a ghetto neighborhood, participants find themselves dealing with some of the problems of the poor. They face the problem of how they are going to invest their potentially productive hours in their neighborhood. Will they go to school, work, hustle, improve their environment, go on welfare, or rest and recreate? In addition to the consideration of these questions there is the added question of how they will live with the other participants, who are often directly affected by each others' decisions. Takes $1-1\frac{2}{3}$ hours with 7-25 players. $20 from Western Publishing Co.

Propaganda

Propaganda teaches people to recognize the persuasive techniques that are used by professionals to form public opinion. The game involves 3-7 players in over 50 techniques; quotations out of context, bargaining appeal, attraction, faulty analogy, and rationalization are a few. Players have 245 samples of writings from advertisers, lawyers, and politicians, etc., to analyze. They must try to separate the emotional appeal from the factual content in each. They label each example, basing each judgment on given definitions of techniques. After the decisions are tallied, players find they are either majority voters or minority voters. Each of the minority voters can accept the popular vote or try to persuade the popular voters to change their opinions. Points are won by accurately labeling, correctly challenging, or effectively persuading. Toward the end of the game players can provide their own examples from newspapers, television, magazines, and political speeches.

Available from Maret Co., 1111 Maple Ave., Turtle Creek, Pa. 15145.

Sensitivity

Sensitivity is a game for adults who wish to communicate with each other, perhaps in ways they didn't realize were possible.

Each player receives approximately 20 clues into the life of a fictional character from a folder containing letters, memos, bills, and phone messages supposedly taken from the desk of the fabricated character. He is given five minutes to study his folder and to take on the identity of the troubled individual.

Each player gives a brief autobiography to the group. A dialogue among the players develops, and participants become involved with their characters, while at the same time getting insights into their own behavior. Players receive indications of their impact on the others through red anger cards and blue sympathy cards.

There are no winners or losers, no points; the fun is in the playing and complete involvement the game produces. For 5-8 adults; available for $10 from Sensitivity Games, Inc., 9 Newbury St., Boston, Mass. 02116.

Squirms

Squirms are role-playing situations printed on papers (pink for girls, blue for boys) inside a can. The role player (called in the instruction "me alone") picks one squirm and reads it to the group; one other role player is the antagonist. The situations are really squirmy. For example: "You just chickened out of a date with a boy and had your mother tell him you were ill. The next day you meet him at a tennis court." Or another: "You are asked by a friend to buy a camera which you really do want at a very cheap price. You finally find out that the camera is lifted from a big department store, but are still tempted to buy it from your friend." To make matters even more interesting, the other role player is "another person who has been shoplifting." The can of squirms comes complete with a leader's guide and discussion questions for slow starters, directions for making the role playing into a game with two teams, a scoring system, twenty squirms, and a scoring pad and pencil. Price is $5 each, 2-pack for $8, 6-pack for $12.

Starpower

Starpower is an excellent game requiring only colored chips or pieces of paper and an instruction book to play. Eighteen participants is the minimum to make the game interesting; about 30 is the ideal with the maximum somewhere around 40.

Chips with varied values are given out, and through trading, players are given the chance to progress through a three-level society—the poor, the middle class, and the upper, ruling class. As the game begins, group members do not know which class they belong to. After trading and a public listing of scores, they soon realize what their station in society is.

After a few rounds of trading, the leading team is given the privilege of making the rules for the remainder of the game. They most often make rules designed to maintain their own privileged status. How the other teams react is left to them.

All sorts of things can happen once the ruling class instigates oppressive rules. Some lower-class members will look for loopholes in the rules; others will come to the teacher for a way out; others will run; and still others will fight to try to make deals.

The game provokes endless discussion not only about the game but about the parallels between the game and reality. A copy of the instructions and a teacher's guide can be obtained for $3 from Similie II, P.O. Box 1023, La Jolla, Calif. 92037.

Sunshine

This game simulates a typical American community of 50,000 moving toward and through a racial crisis. Because of their "birth" as Negro or white at the beginning of the simulation and because of what happens to them in their simulated community, students become concerned about the racial issues seething around them.

The game is fairly elaborate and requires careful study and planning. Available as an instruction booklet for $10 from Interact, P.O. Box 262, Lakeside, Calif. 92040.

Teaching Achievement Motivation

A series of educational games is used in *Teaching Achievement Motivation,* but its basic idea goes beyond simulation gaming. The materials in this kit were developed in the Achievement Motivation Development Project at Harvard University and include a 200-page basic manual, which presents the philosophy and technique of motivation education, teaching guides, student booklets, strategies, and exercises.

The approach is a planned, highly structured attempt to let people experience and understand one basic human concern—the desire to strive for excellence. The aim of the series of games and discussions is to help people become motivated so they can fulfill their own life goals.

The kit or materials titled *The N-Ach Mini-Packet* can be ordered for $10.95 from St. John's University Press, Dept. of Learning Resources, Collegeville, Minn. 56321.

The Value Game

This game is based on the belief that people often have values in their minds that are ideally held only as long as they are separated from real situations. Once a decision must actually be made, ideal values are altered and changed to meet the occasion. The game is a discussion simulation about value systems, urban ethics, and pluralistic ethical systems. It can be played by 15-40 players and takes 1-1½ hours.

Further information from John Washburn.

The Youth Culture Game

This is an elaborate game for 20-80 players. It is a multi-media simulation, enabling players to take on roles in both youth and adult cultures: school, political activist organizations, army, street gangs, communes, police, etc. The game is led by six or more youths and advisors and is designed to be a learning experience for adults and an occasion for youths to discover where they are in the emerging youth culture.

The game requires elaborate preparations, several rooms, and a number of inexpensive props. The instruction book and resource guide to the game sell for $15 from Urbandyne, 5659 South Woodlawn Ave., Chicago, Ill. 60637.